W9-AQQ-386

ENOUGH BULL

EN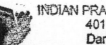UGH
BULL

HOW TO RETIRE WELL WITHOUT THE STOCK MARKET, MUTUAL FUNDS, OR EVEN AN INVESTMENT ADVISOR

Second Edition

David Trahair

WILEY

Cover Design: Wiley

Published by John Wiley & Sons, Inc., Hoboken, New Jersey.

Published simultaneously in Canada.

For general information on our other products and services or for technical support, please contact our Customer Care Department within the United States at (800) 762-2974, outside the United States at (317) 572-3993 or fax (317) 572-4002.

Wiley publishes in a variety of print and electronic formats and by print-on-demand. Some material included with standard print versions of this book may not be included in e-books or in print-on-demand. If this book refers to media such as a CD or DVD that is not included in the version you purchased, you may download this material at http://booksupport.wiley.com. For more information about Wiley products, visit www.wiley.com.

Library of Congress Cataloging-in-Publication Data:

ISBN 9781118994177 (Hardcover)
ISBN 9781118994191 (ePDF)
ISBN 9781118994184 (ePub)

Printed in the United States of America

10 9 8 7 6 5 4 3 2 1

CONTENTS

CONTENTS

CONTENTS

CONTENTS

CONTENTS

CONTENTS

ABOUT THE AUTHOR

DAVID TRAHAIR, CPA, CA, is a speaker, national bestselling author and financial columnist for CPA Magazine. His other books include Smoke and Mirrors: Financial Myths That Will Ruin Your Retirement Dreams, Crushing Debt: Why Canadians Should Drop Everything and Pay Off Debt and Cash Cows, Pigs and Jackpots: The Simplest Personal Finance Strategy Ever. He is known for his ability to explain the often-confusing world of personal finance in plain English. Canadians appreciate his no-nonsense style and the fact that his views are totally independent because he does not sell any financial products. He currently operates his own financial consulting firm and gives seminars on his books to accountants in B.C., Alberta, Saskatchewan, Manitoba, Ontario and Nova Scotia.

ACKNOWLEDGEMENTS

I'd like to start off by thanking the two people that are responsible for the creation of this book. Those people are my literary agent, Hilary McMahon of Westwood Creative Artists, and Karen Milner of John Wiley & Sons Canada, Ltd., my publisher. If not for Hilary's belief in the idea and Karen's enthusiasm for seeing it get into print, you wouldn't be holding it right now.

I'd like to dedicate it to two other significant people in my life. First, to my mom, Florence Trahair, who passed away in 2008 at age eighty-two. She was always my biggest supporter. I felt her presence as I wrote this book. And second, to my father-in-law, Jack Baxter, who passed away in 2006 at age sixty-eight. Jack was one of my best buddies. He taught me how to enjoy life. I know he enjoyed each and every day of his.

And much thanks to Tula Batanchiev and Lia Ottaviano at Wiley for all the hard work in making this second edition a reality.

INTRODUCTION

Welcome to the second edition! A lot has happened since the first edition of this book came out in early 2009. As I read through the first edition to see what needed updated, it occurred to me that my opinions haven't changed. I still stand by everything I said the first time – the stock market is no place to trust your hard-earned retirement savings in.

But some sections needed updated. For example the whole chapter on CPP is revised for the new rules that came into effect after edition one was published. And here's a bonus: this edition now includes step-by-step instructions for you to compute exactly how much CPP pension you can expect.

Ok, let's start at the beginning.

The period of time we lived through in 2008 and 2009 shifted the financial world on its axis. The old rules regarding personal finance are now history, as in obsolete.

This happened in the last quarter, the autumn of 2008. Let's call it "The Fall of 2008."

THE FALL OF 2008

During this period financial institutions that had existed for more than a century simply disappeared. World stock markets tanked. Entire investment portfolios were devastated. Retirement dreams wiped out.

What this series of events has done is show quite clearly the naked truth: traditional financial planning techniques don't work. In fact, if we had done the opposite of what the "experts" have told us to do to get ahead financially, we would be far better off today. Here are some of the past theories and the new reality:

- Trust the stock market to make us wealthy? Never again.
- Pay our investment advisor a fee of over 2% a year to try to beat the market? I don't think so.
- Risk our home trying to "make our mortgage tax deductible" by investing in mutual funds? Please, give me a break.
- Maximize our RRSP contributions religiously each and every year … and also save 10% of our income above that. You must be kidding, right?
- Borrow to invest – "leverage" our way to riches? Forget it. Many have tried; you can now find most of them in the poorhouse.
- Skip a cup of coffee to get rich automatically? Yeah, right.

I am not opposed to capitalism. We need efficient stock markets so that entrepreneurial people can grow businesses that flourish – businesses that create great products, deliver excellent services, hire good people, make profits and pay taxes.

The problem is that, obviously, markets have not been regulated satisfactorily. Businesses, especially financial ones in the United States, have been allowed to run rampant in the quest for riches. Thousands of intelligent, well-educated people making six-figure salaries and multi-million dollar bonuses spent years creating complex financial products that were sold to unsuspecting members of the public.

Ever heard of collateralized debt obligations? Mortgage-backed securities? Non-bank asset-backed commercial paper? What about income trusts? Or even mutual funds?

These complex instruments made many people rich. The people that invented them. The people that re-packaged them. And the people that sold them.

Unfortunately, the vast majority of people that bought into them got screwed. There's the homeowner with no job and no money who was convinced to take out a mortgage on his home and ended up losing it. There's the government, and the taxpayers, forced to shell out billions of dollars to buy into financial houses-of-cards just to keep them afloat. And of course, there's anyone who holds investments in these worthless companies.

ANGRY YET?

I am, and that's why I wrote this book. To give you hope. To show you that there is a way to get ahead financially. And you don't have to be a genius or trust a financial expert to get you there.

I am going to show you how you can do it with a guarantee that in the future your investments will never decline. I can say that because we won't be using the stock market. We won't even be using mutual funds. It is so easy to follow you won't even need to think about it for more than a few hours a year. It is so simple that once implemented you may not even need an investment advisor.

It's the plan laid out in this book that you can read in less than one day. After you read it you'll be able to explain it fully in five minutes.

WHY I WROTE THIS BOOK

I wrote it because I have received a lot of emails like this:

> Good morning, David. I have just finished reading your book *Smoke and Mirrors: Financial Myths That Will Ruin Your Retirement Dreams* and I couldn't agree with you more. I am, however, concerned about my daughter and son-in-law who have this mantra that everything goes into the RRSP. I need to educate them and your line of thinking is what I need to approach them with.

> While my children are quite well off, I am scraping by – having lost most of my portfolio in the recent stock market crash while my husband was going through a major cancer operation and my portfolio was not on my mind and, sad to say, nor on my broker's mind. The good thing is hubby survived, but our belts are very tight as a result of looking the other way for even a few days.

> Joanne

This email arrived in January of 2005. The stock market crash she was talking about was the crash of March of 2000. In 2008 I started to hear more such stories.

YOUR RETIREMENT JOURNEY

But does the whole idea of financial planning need to be so complex? If you listen to all the experts, you'll often end up confused. You may be thinking:

- My investment advisor is telling me I have to invest more but my existing savings have just gotten whacked in the market and I still haven't even recovered the losses – isn't this advice like throwing good money after bad?
- Getting my finances in order is going to be painful. Forget it. I want to live now!
- This is all so depressing. I never seem to be making much progress.
- All the standard retirement advice says that I'm on the wrong track. Jeepers, my unused RRSP room is huge!
- Personal finances are very complex; I can never get a good handle on what is going on with my money even after talking to my broker.
- I may never be able to afford to retire!

You know what? It doesn't have to be confusing or complicated. It never used to be – mutual funds only became popular at the end of the twentieth century, RRSPs were only introduced in 1957 and capital gains tax didn't even exist before 1972. The truth is that the whole subject of personal finance has been made complicated because it makes money for the people that run the financial system. It is designed to be complex so that these financial types can continue to earn six-figure salaries – off the hard-earned savings of the little guy and gal.

Let's make an analogy shall we? They want us to believe that the typical journey to retirement is like a trip down a river. A river is the best way to get there – walking is too slow. It's a complicated journey, so you'll obviously need a guide, right?

DOWN THE RIVER

We arrive at our advisor's headquarters to learn about the trip we are about to take.

"Welcome friends, you've come to the right place! We have been in business for more than twenty years and we know rivers like the back of our hands. Trust us – we'll get you to your destination safely."

The advisor goes on to describe the trip.

"Rivers are different and you never really know what to expect. We have accompanied our clients on thousands of river trips. We know what to expect! We can guide you through rough waters. Don't worry – let our experience be your guide!"

"Now step into the next office, where we'll teach you all about what you're likely to see and experience during the journey."

So you step through the door where you are asked to sign the "Know Your Client" form. This form is necessary for the advisor. It proves you OK'd some level of risk taking. If you read the fine print, you'll see that the onus is on you to protect yourself.

Now, in this case, the advisor doesn't know which river you're going to be travelling down. If he has had little experience, he may have only travelled down easy flowing rivers with nice scenery.

The more experienced advisors know that most trips are never soothing for long. They know the trip may be anything but.

If they were forced into full disclosure, they'd have to warn you of the truth:

Most retirement journeys using the stock market are like a journey down the river – the Niagara River!

UH-OH, IT'S THE NIAGARA RIVER

Here's what you should know before you begin the journey. According to Niagara Parks, an agency of the Government of Ontario, the Niagara River is 58 kilometres long, beginning in Lake Erie and ending in Lake Ontario. The elevation between the lakes is about 99 Metres (326 feet). About half of that elevation change occurs at one spot – Niagara Falls.

At Grand Island, the river divides into the west channel, known as the Canadian or Chippawa Channel, and the east channel, known as the American or Tonawanda Channel.

INTRODUCTION

The Canadian Horseshoe Falls drops an average of 57 metres (188 feet) while the American Falls ranges from 21 to 34 metres (70 to 110 feet). That measurement is taken from the top of the falls to the top of the rock pile at the base, called the Talus Slope. The height of the American Falls from the top of the falls to the river below the rocks is the same as the Canadian Horseshoe Falls.

Sections of the river move quite slowly, but the speed of the water in the rapids just above the falls reaches 40 kilometres per hour (25 miles per hour). Speeds of over 100 kilometres per hour (60 miles per hour) have been recorded at the falls themselves. At the Whirlpool Rapids below the falls, water travels at about 50 kilometres per hour (30 miles per hour).

The great volume of water going over the falls is forced into a narrow gorge called the Great Gorge, where the Whirlpool Rapids are formed. The water surface here drops 15 metres (50 feet) and the water speeds reach 9 metres per second (30 feet per second). The whirlpool is a basin formed where the river takes a sharp right turn. The actual whirlpool is created by the "reversal phenomenon." Here, the water travels over the rapids and enters the pool, then travels counterclockwise past the natural outlet. When the exiting water tries to cut across itself to reach the outlet, pressure builds up and forces the water under the incoming stream. The swirling waters create a vortex or whirlpool.

Beyond the whirlpool is another set of rapids that drops approximately 12 metres (40 feet).

"Are you ready?" your advisor then asks. "Let's jump into the boat then, shall we?"

Assume your journey to retirement is the 58-kilometre stretch from Lake Erie to Lake Ontario along the Niagara River. It would be an exciting trip, wouldn't it? Some parts would be calm and slow, others bumpy and very fast. There would be smooth sections and jaw-dropping plunges. There would be parts where you'd feel like you were going nowhere – spinning in circles. There'd possibly even be some rocky sections. Doesn't that sound like the typical trip to retirement using the stock market?

RETIREMENT JOURNEY: PLAN B

But is a trip down Niagara the only way to get to Lake Ontario? In personal finance terms, is trusting the stock market to carry our retirement nest egg to our destination the best way to go?

I don't think so. Personally I'd rather avoid the jaw-dropping plunges. Decisions like whether to go over the Canadian Falls, or the smaller American Falls with the rock slope at the bottom, are decisions I don't care to make!

I also don't like the idea of spinning around a whirlpool at 50 kilometers an hour hoping I don't drown. And I'd prefer a smooth ride to one that might throw me out of the boat.

HERE'S WHAT THEY DON'T WANT YOU TO KNOW

Well, here's what they don't want you to know: you don't need to use the Niagara River. You don't need the stock market or mutual funds. You don't need to risk your financial life going over spectacular plunges or stagnating for endless periods of time going around in circles hoping you won't go under in the process.

You can take the guaranteed route – the safe road – and this book will show you how.

PART ONE THE ANTIDOTE - A SIX POINT PLAN FOR FINANCIAL FREEDOM

The Antidote is a simple plan. It'll only take you a few minutes to read the six-point synopsis below.

But here is the best thing about it: You don't need to follow it in order. You don't even need to religiously follow each one of the six points. The fact of the matter is that if you stick to just one of the points, you'll probably make a significant improvement in your personal finances.

Follow it all and you can rest easy knowing that your retirement nest egg will never decline, even if your bank goes out of business.

Here it is.

1. AVOID PERSONAL FINANCIAL DISASTERS

- Never touch anything that cannot be simply explained to you in plain English.
- Don't invest in anything that is not guaranteed by the government.
- Never borrow to invest.
- Avoid complicated investment schemes. If it sounds too good to be true, it is.

2. YOU DON'T NEED THE STOCK MARKET OR MUTUAL FUNDS

- The truth is that you don't need to risk your hard-earned money in the stock market and you don't need mutual funds.
- You can use 100% government-guaranteed investment certificates to achieve your goals without the risk of losing your shirt.
- If you want to take a chance, buy a lottery ticket.

3. BUY A HOME AND PAY OFF THE MORTGAGE

- Decide if you can afford a house and, if you can, buy one.
- Do the calculation of how many years it will take to pay off the mortgage and do it before you retire.
- Never risk your home for any kind of investment idea, no matter what.

4. REDUCING EXPENSES DOESN'T HAVE TO BE PAINFUL

- Focus on two of your biggest expenses – income taxes and interest on your debt.
- Pay to have your family's personal income tax returns prepared by a qualified expert.

- Pay extra to have that expert analyze your family situation to minimize your tax bill by income splitting, etc.
- Find out what your credit rating is and improve it.
- Get at least three quotes on any debt that you get into.

5. FORGET RRSPs UNTIL YOUR DEBT IS PAID OFF (THE OPPORTUNITY ZONE)

- Do not even think about saving for retirement until you have paid off student loans and bought a home.
- Pay off the mortgage before investing another dime in an RRSP.
- Never borrow to invest in an RRSP.

6. ASK YOURSELF IF YOU REALLY NEED AN INVESTMENT ADVISOR

- If you've got a bad one, find a good one.
- If you can't find a good one, simplify your finances so you don't need one at all.

1

AVOID PERSONAL FINANCIAL DISASTERS

In the mid-eighties I took one of those personality tests that determine what type of person you are, what your strengths and weaknesses are and what type of career you'd be suited for. The results were not too surprising: I was basically a pretty normal person, pretty good at math, probably never going to be a great artist or preacher.

But then, at the end of the session, the person giving me the results told me something that has turned out to be one of the most important pieces of information that I have ever received in my life. It was this:

Dave, you can't tell when people are lying to you.

What? You mean I can't tell by looking directly into someone's eyes and monitoring their body language whether they are telling me the truth? Exactly.

And you know what? Neither can you.

Think about it. Ever watched a great actor in a movie? There are great actors all around us each and every day. The problem is that some of them want to rip us off.

I was fortunate enough to learn this lesson in my twenties and it has stood me in good stead when it comes to investing, as well as life in general. I don't assume everyone I meet is lying to me. For example,

I have known my buddy Stu for over thirty years and I know I can trust him because he has never once lied to me.

On the other hand, I initially do not trust people I meet for the first time, even if they have been referred by a friend or client.

Unfortunately, many people did not take the personality test in their twenties that I did. They learned the hard way that many people can't be trusted. One of the early examples when it comes to investing rip-offs was that of Charles Ponzi.

THE PONZI SCHEME

This scheme is often at the root of many investment scams today.

Charles Ponzi (pronounced "pon-zee") was born in Italy in 1882 as Carlo Ponzi. He grew up there and emigrated to the U.S. in 1903 at the age of twenty-one.

His first stop? Canada. He went to Montreal, where he was convicted of forgery in 1908 and sentenced to three years in prison. After his early release for good behaviour he was soon arrested on immigration charges for trying to assist five other people get into the U.S. illegally. He was jailed again in 1910.

After his release, he spent time in several cities and held various jobs, including dishwasher, waiter and office clerk. He eventually settled down in Boston in 1917, where he worked in clerical office jobs.

On December 26, 1919, Ponzi established a company called the Securities Exchange Company. He had hit upon an idea to make himself rich. It had to do with postal international reply coupons (IRCs). These are coupons that can be exchanged for one or more postage stamps for the minimum postage for an airmail letter to be returned to any other country that is a member of the Universal Postal Union. The purpose of an IRC is to send someone a letter in another country with sufficient postage for them to send a reply. For letters in the same country you can simply use a self-addressed stamped envelope, but for mailings to other countries, using an IRC does away with the need to use foreign postage or currency.

Ponzi claimed that he could make money by taking advantage of different postal and exchange rates in different countries. For example, he claimed he could send $1 to Italy and with the IRC he could buy

$3.30 worth of stamps in Boston. He promised a 50% return in 90 days. In the beginning he actually did pay that rate of return – often in only forty-five days.

To many people, it sounded like a good idea. The money started to flow in.

Within a few months people began lining up at his company's door. Thousands of people invested their hard-earned savings. At its peak the company was bringing in more than $1 million a week, and that was in the early 1920s.

The problem was that he never really bought the IRCs or even attempted to make any money for the investors. He simply paid the return out of the money that other investors had put in, and he just spent the rest.

It was so devastating that even the U.S. Securities and Exchange Commission (SEC) devotes a page to it on its website.

Here's what it says:

Ponzi schemes are a type of illegal pyramid scheme named for Charles Ponzi, who duped thousands of New England residents into investing in a postage stamp speculation scheme back in the 1920s. Ponzi thought he could take advantage of differences between U.S. and foreign currencies used to buy and sell international mail coupons. Ponzi told investors that he could provide a 40% return in just 90 days compared with 5% for bank savings accounts. Ponzi was deluged with funds from investors, taking in $1 million during one three-hour period – and this was 1921! Though a few early investors were paid off to make the scheme look legitimate, an investigation found that Ponzi had only purchased about $30 worth of the international mail coupons.

Decades later, the Ponzi scheme continues to work on the "rob-Peter-to-pay-Paul" principle, as money from new investors is used to pay off earlier investors until the whole scheme collapses.

(U.S. Securities and Exchange Commission, "ponzi" schemes.
http://www.sec.gov/answers/ponzi.htm.)

How could people fall for a scheme that promised such huge returns in so little time? Well, they did, and they continue to do so.

If you look up Charles Ponzi in Wikipedia, under "Similar Schemes" you'll see a new name: Bernard Madoff – Bernie to his friends.

BERNIE MADOFF

Bernard L. Madoff was arrested on December 11, 2008 by U.S. Federal authorities in New York City on charges that he perpetuated a massive securities fraud on the investors in his investment hedge fund. Estimates of the losses ranged up to US$65 billion. We now know that this was the total inflated market value of the investors' money. According to recent federal filings Bernard L. Madoff Investment Securities LLC, the firm Madoff started in 1960, actually held $17 billion in over two dozen funds.

A *New York Times* article dated December 11, 2008[1] quotes an associate director of enforcement for the U.S. SEC as calling it "a stunning fraud that appears to be of epic proportions."

The funds had been widely marketed to wealthy investors, hedge funds and other large institutional investors for decades. In fact there were approximately 77 "feeder funds" all over the world bringing in money that was forwarded to Madoff. Madoff's funds were popular because they promised high returns with low fees.

It seems that part of the reason that this scheme lasted so long was that the returns promised and reported seem to be high but not outrageously so. For example, one of Madoff's funds, the Fairfield Sentry Limited Fund, reported assets of US$7.3 billion in October 2008 and claimed to have paid more than 11% interest each year during its fifteen-year track record, according to the *Times* article.

I guess Bernie learned his lessons from Charles Ponzi well.

How did he do this? How did he convince dozens of sophisticated investors and financial institutions to trust him with their funds?

Well, one of the reasons is that he appeared to be a nice guy, with little or no ego. He used to tell interviewers that he got his initial

---

[1] (http://www.nytimes.com/2008/12/12/business/12scheme.html)

earnings to start his firm in 1960 by working as a lifeguard at city beaches and installing underground sprinkler systems.

In fact, I just watched a thirty-four-minute video of Madoff that was posted on YouTube, entitled "Bernie Madoff on the modern stock market." It was a roundtable discussion on October 20, 2007, shortly after the subprime mortgage crises started in the U.S. with stock markets riding high. One of his employees, a computer programming expert, sits beside him throughout.

During the video, he exudes charm. He said he employs highly educated MBAs, but he himself was "happy to graduate college." At one point he hired engineers from MIT to help with the computer trading models the firm employs but they "think too much." That gets a laugh from the audience.

He seems to know what he is talking about. He comes across as an expert. He never interrupts anyone. He'd be the kind of guy you'd want to introduce your kids to if they wanted to get into the investment industry. Well, except for the fact that you now know that he is a consummate con artist.

A couple of the most interesting comments actually come at the end from the audience. One individual in the investment industry makes the point that most people who invest big money in the stock market actually made their fortune somewhere else – in an actual business – and bring the money to the market in an attempt to make more. They did not become wealthy by buying stocks!

His employee, a guy who at the time made his living investing, makes the point that the market is fuelled by greed and fear. He goes on to talk about greed being a slow process, and fear happening fast. When markets are going up month by month, year by year, people get in. Some start early, some late. Some invest a lot, some not so much. When things go bad, the "herd mentality" causes people to panic. The fear of losing money causes everyone to act. They all sell. Markets crash, and they crash quickly.

Yeah, we know.

I realize that Bernie Madoff is an American dealing with many wealthy investors, so you may not be able to relate to the plight of the people who trusted him. But, con artists don't just exist in New York. They live everywhere, even in Canada.

OUR VERY OWN CANADIAN FRAUD

The Eron Mortgage fraud happened in British Columbia. That is not a typo. It's not the "Enron" fraud. It's our own very particular Canadian Fraud.

What's different about this fraud is that a detailed study of the ins and outs of how and why it happened was performed. And the results are intriguing.

The report is titled "Eron Mortgage Study." The principal researcher was Neil Boyd, LL.B., LL.M., Professor and Associate Director, School of Criminology at Simon Fraser University. The study, conducted in 2004 and 2005, is the first comprehensive study of an investment fraud and includes responses from more than 2,200 Eron Mortgage investors. This was a detailed project. Researchers reviewed relevant existing research on investment fraud; reviewed the B.C. Securities Commission findings on the case, held several focus groups; and distributed two sets of surveys – an initial one to 520 random Eron investors, and a refined, final version to 1,765 investors. They also conducted 180 telephone interviews and had face-to-face meetings with regulators, legal counsel, accountants and other experts in securities legislation and investor fraud.

The first thing that strikes you is the sheer number of victims. Roughly 2,800 people became prey to this one scheme and this is just one private market deal in one Canadian province.

The second thing that hits you is the absolutely devastating affect that losing money in this scam had on people. Consider this quote received from an Eron investor:

It made sense to me. Joe Blow has a piece of property but can't proceed, because of not having capital to proceed. Therefore he borrows money at high interest until he gets the infrastructure together for this project that he's hoping to have happen. As soon as he's got something, the banks or someone else can mortgage it for him, and he would pay back the high interest loan.

A friend of a friend that told me about Eron, and at the time I was a struggling single parent, and he encouraged me and *an awful lot of others to invest in this ... so I invested all the savings I had – about $14,000. All I remember is that I was a single parent and was struggling. I know that to some people the $14,000 wasn't much, but it was disastrous to me.*

That's often the "hook": the ideas seem to make some logical sense.

The other thing to take careful note of is the personal connection angle. Boyd's research on the dynamics of victimization indicated that frauds are most likely to be successful if the victim had some kind of personal tie to the con artist. In most cases, the initial contact was in person or through a third party, television or the media as opposed to mail or telephone.

What Did the "Average" Victim Look Like?

There was no common attribute among survey respondents, no single "flaw" that researchers could find. Most (61%) of the investors were male and working at the time of the investment. The average age of the Eron investors was fifty-five at the time of first investment, with approximately 64% over age forty-five at that time.

They seemed to be no better educated or more affluent than the average British Columbian of similar age. About one-third had a University education, one-third had some college or post-secondary training and the rest were either high school graduates or did not complete secondary education.

The majority were not wealthy. At the time, about two-thirds had total annual household incomes of less than $75,000 with only 12% reporting that it was over $100,000. This is similar to the average Canadian.

The majority (60%) had a household net worth of under $250,000 excluding their principal residence.

Almost half (48%) considered themselves conservative investors and fully 78% admitted they were not "very knowledgeable of the securities market and mortgage investments."

The study seems to confirm the desire to attain wealth the "easy" way. While 62% thought the Eron investment was no-risk or low-risk, the number one reason people were attracted was the high guaranteed rate of return. Sophisticated investors would know there is no such thing as a high guaranteed rate of return. In this case, 34% of the investors did not even know they were investing – they thought they were providing a loan with a guaranteed rate of return.

How Did Investors Become Involved in Eron?

Most of them heard about Eron through family and friends; however, Eron seminars, brokers, newspaper and television ads were also important. Most respondents (55%) read the Eron investor prospectus, but it is not clear that would have done any good as there is no proof it was an honest document. Since this was not a public company, it did not have to file a prospectus with the B.C. Securities Commission.

What Steps Did They Take Before Investing?

Less than half the investors took additional steps beyond reading the prospectus. These steps included viewing photographs of the project, consulting with family and friends who were involved, speaking with other investors or visiting the Eron offices. It is not clear, though, if this would have done any good in this case, as it was a bogus operation.

Very few people took steps that may have warned them early enough. Only 13% reviewed audited financial statements, 11% sought independent professional advice, 7% actually visited the properties and only 6% checked with regulatory agencies.

Only 2% of the investors bothered to check the backgrounds of the two principals that invented the scheme. If they had, they would have found out that both had been bankrupt before and had a history of failed businesses. This may have been enough to discourage some, but a background check is not a fail-safe way to protect yourself. Remember, Bernie Madoff was the chairman of the NASDAQ stock exchange at one point and had a very good reputation.

Why Did They Invest?

When asked the main purpose of their Eron investment, 58% said to build their retirement savings. The next most common answer, at 19%, was to enhance current lifestyle. This is a significant finding. It means that many people are worried about financing their retirement and are willing to take significant risk to try to solve the problem.

This makes many people pre-disposed to being ripped off. Retiring well involves a bit of work and those who say you can simply hand your money over and walk away knowing you're being well taken care of are probably trying to make money off you.

Where Did They Get the Money?

Tragically, in most cases the money used for investing in the scheme was not from excess savings but from existing retirement savings, mortgages on their homes and loans from financial institutions. Boyd's conclusion is that "a significant number of the investors jeopardized their financial security because of their apparent concerns for their financial futures."

In other words, in pursuit of their goals they ignored point number one of a successful retirement strategy: avoid situations that could lead to personal financial disaster.

The Lessons of Eron

The lessons of Eron are simple:

- **Don't believe anyone who says they can guarantee a high rate of return.** Achieving a high rate of return means accepting risk – the risk that you could lose it all.
- **Knowing someone involved does not help.** In fact, it often does more harm than good. People seem to "let their guard down" when friends or family are involved.
- **Investment education is the best defense.** Trying to blame securities regulators after the loss is essentially a waste of time. Educate and protect yourself – don't get involved in the first place.

- **Check the background of the people involved.** In this case both principals had gone bankrupt before. Would you trust your life savings with someone like that?

EXTRAORDINARY POPULAR DELUSIONS

Beware that disaster can strike even if there is no con artist. People's own lust for wealth can lead to disaster all by itself. All you have to do is think back to the dot-com bubble around the year 2000. People were freely investing in companies that did not have any profits. In fact, many companies did not even have any *revenues*. All they had were ideas. Buying pet food over the Internet anyone?

This is not a new concept. I read a great book called *Extraordinary Popular Delusions and the Madness of Crowds* (Charles Mackay, 1980) that details sixteen different cases of people losing their heads, and then their shirts, over the latest "sure thing."

It includes the tale of Tulipomania, where more than a few lost fortunes on a single tulip bulb! (The story of the merchant who ate a tulip mistaking it for an onion is worth the price of the book).

It also includes the story of the South-Sea Bubble of England in the 1700s, where thousands were left penniless believing the South-Sea Company would make them rich through free trading with the ports of South America. During this period it seemed everyone wanted to invest in almost any idea imaginable to get rich.

One such company's prospectus actually stated its purpose as: "For carrying on an undertaking of great advantage; but nobody to know what it is." The government had to declare it illegal just to prevent people from investing in it!

But probably the most important lesson of the book is what happened after the South-Sea bubble scam had been exposed. Everyone was after the heads of the directors of the South-Sea Company, who by their fraudulent practices had brought the nation to virtual ruin. Here's what Mackay says:

Nobody seemed to imagine that the nation itself was as culpable as the South-Sea Company. Nobody blamed the credulity and avarice of the people – the degrading lust for gain, which had swallowed up every nobler quality in the national character, or the infatuation which had made the multitude run their heads with such frantic eagerness into the net held out for them by scheming projectors. These things were never mentioned. The people were a simple, honest, hard-working people, ruined by a gang of robbers, who were to be hanged, drawn and quartered without mercy

(Charles Mackay, Extraordinary Popular Delusions and the Madness of Crowds [New York: Harmony Books, 1980], 72)

This is an important point that was also made in the Eron Mortgage Study. Sure, there are con artists and there always will be. But the con artists cannot be successful if people don't fall for their schemes.

OTHER POTENTIAL DISASTERS

It's not just chasing the riches promised by schemers that can lead to financial ruin. There are many other potential disasters awaiting Canadians. Here are but a few:

Credit Card Disease

I once had an e-mail from a gentleman whose credit card debt exceeded his family's total annual gross salary. He said they simply could not afford to live without credit cards. While most Canadians aren't in this bad a situation, a large percentage – the card companies say it's approximately 30% – carry a balance month to month. In other words, they spend more than they make, using credit cards to make that possible.

This is not only a waste of money (with interest charges at 20% or more), it can lead to the ultimate personal financial disaster: bankruptcy. But you know what? This is not the credit card companies' fault. And while you could argue that the rates are excessively high, the companies are not forcing consumers to use their cards. The problem is the spending habits of the people.

That's why it's so hard to pay off a credit card balance. You may be able to pay a big chunk down but the additional charges during the last month often offset any paydown. Add the fuel of easy credit card availability and many Canadians are putting their whole financial future at risk.

Taking Out a Mortgage on Your Home to Invest

You could end up losing your investment ... and your house.

The Latest Stock Chase

Many people seem to want to get rich, easily and quickly. What better way than the latest stock market darling? Enron, WorldCom, Nortel, Bre-X anyone? The folly of this strategy usually becomes clear too late.

Trusting Your "Friends"

There are more and more stories surfacing these days about incompetent or even out-and-out fraud by "investment advisors." Now obviously, I don't want to paint all advisors with the same brush, but many people place their retirement in the hands of friends or even relatives that are simply unqualified or even rip-off artists.

Mortgage Fraud

Imagine a senior having paid off the home mortgage, only to have it stolen from her by an unscrupulous thief who registers a mortgage on her property without her knowledge.

HOW TO PREVENT PERSONAL FINANCIAL DISASTERS

You need to have preventative controls in place so you don't get conned. In other words, don't expect a "big brother" to bail you out of a bad decision. In most cases the government, the securities regulators and other watchdogs are not even responsible for trying to recover your money.

Avoid getting sucked in altogether. As Boyd states in his report's conclusion to the Eron Mortgage fraud:

> We can make improvements to regulatory law so that it better protects investors, but it will ultimately be a well-informed and skeptical investor who is less likely to be victimized. (Neil Boyd, Eron Mortgage Study: Final Report [March 31, 2005], 37)

CONCLUSION

Very few people think about this, but avoiding personal financial disasters should be the number one rule of personal finance. Unfortunately, the vast majority of Canadians make at least one major mistake in their personal finances during their life. This often puts them back years and can result in financial devastation.

And just how do they get into these disastrous situations? By falling for the slick sales pitches of unqualified advisors and in some cases outright con artists. The best way to avoid the disasters is to avoid the schemes that can lead to them.

If you take just one thing from this book, make it this one.

YOU DON'T NEED THE STOCK MARKET OR MUTUAL FUNDS

THE WORLDWIDE ECONOMIC MELTDOWN

I started to write this chapter for the first edition of this book on Monday, October 6, 2008. Around noon on that day the S&P/TSX Composite Index had dropped over 1,000 points since the market opened. That was a decline of over 11% in a few hours. By the end of the day the decline had been reduced to 572 points. They say the stock market is volatile, but this is ridiculous. What's worse is that this day had come after already jaw-dropping declines since the index peaked in June of 2008.

In this second edition, I am writing on Wednesday, July 30, 2014. We now have complete information about one of the worst stock market crashes in history, and how the recovery has gone.

Let's start with the bad news.

Check out the chart in Table 2.1 that shows the weekly closing values of the S&P TSX Composite Index from the highest peak it had reached on June 18, 2008 to March 9, 2009.

In that nine-month period almost 50% of the index was lost. In one week alone at the beginning of October, 2008, more than 16% was lost.

TABLE 2.1   S&P TSX Composite Index

Date	Close	Change Since Prior Week	% Change Since Prior Week	% Change Since Peak
18/Jun/08	15,073.13			
20/Jun/08	14,580.67	−492.46	−3.27%	−3.27%
27/Jun/08	14,355.21	−225.46	−1.55%	−4.76%
4/Jul/08	14,010.39	−344.82	−2.40%	−7.05%
11/Jul/08	13,709.10	−301.29	−2.15%	−9.05%
18/Jul/08	13,515.96	−193.14	−1.41%	−10.33%
25/Jul/08	13,378.81	−137.15	−1.01%	−11.24%
1/Aug/08	13,496.53	117.72	0.88%	−10.46%
8/Aug/08	13,341.74	−154.79	−1.15%	−11.49%
15/Aug/08	13,096.70	−245.04	−1.84%	−13.11%
22/Aug/08	13,447.29	350.59	2.68%	−10.79%
29/Aug/08	13,771.25	323.96	2.41%	−8.64%
5/Sep/08	12,816.42	−954.83	−6.93%	−14.97%
12/Sep/08	12,769.58	−46.84	−0.37%	−15.28%
19/Sep/08	12,912.99	143.41	1.12%	−14.33%
26/Sep/08	12,126.00	−786.99	−6.09%	−19.55%
3/Oct/08	10,803.35	−1,322.65	−10.91%	−28.33%
10/Oct/08	9,065.16	−1,738.19	−16.09%	−39.86%
17/Oct/08	9,562.49	497.33	5.49%	−36.56%
24/Oct/08	9,294.09	−268.40	−2.81%	−38.34%
31/Oct/08	9,762.76	468.67	5.04%	−35.23%
7/Nov/08	9,596.21	−166.55	−1.71%	−36.34%
14/Nov/08	9,055.96	−540.25	−5.63%	−39.92%
21/Nov/08	8,155.39	−900.57	−9.94%	−45.89%
28/Nov/08	9,270.62	1,115.23	13.67%	−38.50%
5/Dec/08	8,117.03	−1,153.59	−12.44%	−46.15%
12/Dec/08	8,515.45	398.42	4.91%	−43.51%
19/Dec/08	8,552.00	36.55	0.43%	−43.26%
26/Dec/08	8,310.55	−241.45	−2.82%	−44.87%
2/Jan/09	9,234.11	923.56	11.11%	−38.74%
9/Jan/09	9,085.18	−148.93	−1.61%	−39.73%

TABLE 2.1 (*continued*)

Date	Close	Change Since Prior Week	% Change Since Prior Week	% Change Since Peak
16/Jan/09	8,920.40	−164.78	−1.81%	−40.82%
23/Jan/09	8,627.97	−292.43	−3.28%	−42.76%
30/Jan/09	8,694.90	66.93	0.78%	−42.32%
6/Feb/09	9,008.02	313.12	3.60%	−40.24%
13/Feb/09	8,678.10	−329.92	−3.66%	−42.43%
20/Feb/09	7,949.99	−728.11	−8.39%	−47.26%
27/Feb/09	8,123.02	173.03	2.18%	−46.11%
6/Mar/09	7,591.47	−531.55	−6.54%	−49.64%
9/Mar/09	7,566.94	−24.53	−0.32%	−49.80%

THE UNITED STATES

One of the key indices used to measure the U.S. stock market is the S&P 500 Index. It is a stock price index based on the market capitalization of 500 large U.S. companies and many consider it the best representation of the U.S. stock market. Let's look at Table 2.2 that shows how it fared during the same time period we just looked at for Canada.

During that same nine-month period, the S&P 500 lost almost 50% of its value too. In its worst week in October, 2008, the index lost even more than the Canadian index – just over 18%!

One difference between the two markets to note is that while the S&P TSX Index peaked on June 18, 2008, the S&P 500 Index actually peaked earlier. The highest value it reached before June of 2008 was on October 9, 2007 when it hit 1,565.15.

During this period of stock market devastation, I started receiving phone calls from friends asking for advice. What would you tell a single mother who has just lost half of the hard-earned savings she was counting on to help send her kids to university and for her own retirement?

Tell her to sell and realize her losses with the associated insult that she'd probably have to pay deferred sales charges on her mutual funds to the advisor that steered her wrong in the first place?

TABLE 2.2   S&P 500 Index Weekly June 2008 to June 2009

Date	Close	Change Since Prior Week	% Change Since Prior Week	% Change Since Peak
6/Jun/08	1,360.68			
13/Jun/08	1,360.03	−0.65	−0.05%	−0.05%
20/Jun/08	1,317.93	−42.10	−3.10%	−3.14%
27/Jun/08	1,278.38	−39.55	−3.00%	−6.05%
4/Jul/08	1,262.90	−15.48	−1.21%	−7.19%
11/Jul/08	1,239.49	−23.41	−1.85%	−8.91%
18/Jul/08	1,260.68	21.19	1.71%	−7.35%
25/Jul/08	1,257.76	−2.92	−0.23%	−7.56%
1/Aug/08	1,260.31	2.55	0.20%	−7.38%
8/Aug/08	1,296.32	36.01	2.86%	−4.73%
15/Aug/08	1,298.20	1.88	0.15%	−4.59%
22/Aug/08	1,292.20	−6.00	−0.46%	−5.03%
29/Aug/08	1,282.83	−9.37	−0.73%	−5.72%
5/Sep/08	1,242.31	−40.52	−3.16%	−8.70%
12/Sep/08	1,251.70	9.39	0.76%	−8.01%
19/Sep/08	1,255.08	3.38	0.27%	−7.76%
26/Sep/08	1,213.27	−41.81	−3.33%	−10.83%
3/Oct/08	1,099.23	−114.04	−9.40%	−19.21%
10/Oct/08	899.22	−200.01	−18.20%	−33.91%
17/Oct/08	940.55	41.33	4.60%	−30.88%
24/Oct/08	876.77	−63.78	−6.78%	−35.56%
31/Oct/08	968.75	91.98	10.49%	−28.80%
7/Nov/08	930.99	−37.76	−3.90%	−31.58%
14/Nov/08	873.29	−57.70	−6.20%	−35.82%
21/Nov/08	800.03	−73.26	−8.39%	−41.20%
28/Nov/08	896.24	96.21	12.03%	−34.13%
5/Dec/08	876.07	−20.17	−2.25%	−35.62%
12/Dec/08	879.73	3.66	0.42%	−35.35%
19/Dec/08	887.88	8.15	0.93%	−34.75%
26/Dec/08	872.80	−15.08	−1.70%	−35.86%
2/Jan/09	931.80	59.00	6.76%	−31.52%

TABLE 2.2 (*continued*)

Date	Close	Change Since Prior Week	% Change Since Prior Week	% Change Since Peak
9/Jan/09	890.35	−41.45	−4.45%	−34.57%
16/Jan/09	850.12	−40.23	−4.52%	−37.52%
23/Jan/09	831.95	−18.17	−2.14%	−38.86%
30/Jan/09	825.88	−6.07	−0.73%	−39.30%
6/Feb/09	868.60	42.72	5.17%	−36.16%
13/Feb/09	826.84	−41.76	−4.81%	−39.23%
20/Feb/09	770.05	−56.79	−6.87%	−43.41%
27/Feb/09	735.09	−34.96	−4.54%	−45.98%
6/Mar/09	683.38	−51.71	−7.03%	−49.78%

Or maybe, tell her to hold on? That the stock market will come back eventually as it always used to?

THE RECOVERY

In the first edition of this book, released in 2009, I asked a question about how long the markets would take to recover. The answer was that I had no idea. Now we know.

The S&P TSX Composite Index originally peaked on June 18, 2008 at 15,073.13. It reached that peak again exactly six years later to the day – on June 18, 2014 when it hit 15,109.25. That is an average annual rate of return of 14.83% over the five years from the low value of 7,566.94 reached on March 9, 2009. What an amazing rate of return, right? Well yes, but that's only if you started investing in March, 2009.

Look at it this way. If your portfolio of TSX Index stocks was worth $100,000 on June 18, 2008, it was only worth $50,200 on March 9, 2009. You had to wait six years to get back to the $100,000 you started with, and that is ignoring any investment fees and taxes. That is the problem with percentages and ratios, it can take your eye off what's really important – how much is your portfolio worth in dollars.

The U.S. recovery was faster than the Canadian recovery. As I have mentioned, the S&P 500 Index reached its all-time high to that point of 1,565.15 on October 9, 2007. On June 6, 2008 it was 1,360.68. It reached that level again on April 29, 2011 when it got to 1,363.61. Over the next year it declined again and didn't get back to that level again until February 17, 2012 when it was 1,361.23. It's had its ups-and-downs since then but as of July 24, 2014 it was sitting at the highest level it has ever reached - 1,987.98.

With both markets at peak levels, how confident are you that the good times will last? When will the next crash happen that takes your dreams with it? Again, I have to answer "I don't know." But one thing's for sure – it will happen again. It's just a matter of time.

This is another perfect example of the risk of ignoring point number one of The Antidote – avoid personal financial disasters.

So if this can happen in Canada as well as the U.S., what is the answer? For me, the answer is to swear to never let it happen again. And that can only be achieved by ignoring the stock market, mutual funds and equities of any kind when it comes to personal finances.

Yes, you read that correctly. No more sleepless nights worrying about what is going to happen tomorrow. Put an end to making the investment industry rich off your hard work. Keep what you earn and never again let it evaporate into thin air.

And this book will tell you how to do it.

WHAT CAUSED THE MELTDOWN

The blame gets laid on the U.S. subprime mortgage crisis. For years in the U.S., aggressive mortgage companies pushed mortgages on U.S. consumers who could not afford them. The mortgage sellers would make fees from getting the mortgage in place regardless of the chances of future payment. Combine this with consumers anxious to keep up with the Joneses and you got a toxic brew.

These mortgages were deemed "subprime" because they were issued to people with a less than prime credit rating.

There was even a new concepts created: "stated income mortgages" or "liar loans." People were allowed to apply for mortgages based on just filling in a form stating how much their income was. There was no checking to see if they really did earn what they said they did.

What allowed this problem to spread to a worldwide problem was what happened next. Financial institutions bundled thousands of these subprime mortgages into bonds and sold them to investment banks. The investment banks then repackaged them and resold them as "collateralized debt obligations" or CDOs. These low-grade, high-risk investments were often highly rated, many of them the best you can get – AAA – by the credit rating agencies. Organizations all over the world began buying them.

It was great while it lasted – mortgage grantors made good commissions and fees. Consumers maxed out the amount they could borrow based on ever-rising housing prices. They spent the money on whatever they wanted. Retailers, car manufacturers and dealers loved it, too. But when U.S. house prices started to fall, the wheels came off.

The investment banks began to realize that their own holdings of toxic CDOs were worth a lot less than they paid for them. One of them – Lehman Brothers Holdings Inc. – went bankrupt. All the others were forced to be bought out by another regular bank or, in the case of Morgan Stanley and Goldman Sachs Group Inc., converted into traditional deposit-taking banks.

Merrill Lynch & Co., Inc. was bought by Bank of America in an all-stock deal worth US$50 billion. The deal valued Merrill Lynch at US$29 a share – a 70% premium to its share value at the time - although it had been trading as high as US$50 in May 2008 and US$90. a share at the beginning of January 2007.

If you look at their consolidated balance sheet at June 27, 2008 (unaudited), which I am right now, it's not hard to see why Merrill Lynch was in trouble.

They had US$966 billion in total assets and US$931 billion in total liabilities, leaving total shareholders' equity of US$35 billion. The problem lay in the fact that a lot of their assets were considered "trading assets," that are required to be listed at fair market value for accounting purposes as follows:

Derivative contracts	$86 billion
Mortgages, debt, and asset-backed	$29 billion
Goodwill and other intangible assets	$5 billion

These three items of the twenty different types of assets on their balance sheet are not the type of things you can simply cash in to pay your bills. They are complex instruments that fluctuate in value. After things began going south, it didn't take long for the decline in the asset values to exceed shareholders' equity – the entire value of the company. Merrill and the other investment banks essentially became insolvent.

THE VICIOUS SPIRAL

Please take what I've got to say in context. I am not a macro-economic theory expert. I have not studied world finance or even worked in the banking sector. I am just a simple-minded accountant, but I think we've got a huge problem here and it's not just about the stock market.

The problem we have now is not going to go away quickly. The way I see it is that reality has finally caught up with traditional economic theory. In other words, the laws of physics have caught up with the laws of economics. Let me explain.

The old formula saw lots of financially educated people make lots of money by designing complicated financial products to sell to people that didn't understand them. They took huge bonuses as they made money for their firms.

For example, it is been reported that the management of Merrill Lynch in the U.S. decided to hand out million-dollar bonuses in 2008 earlier than usual - just before they were forced to be bought out by the Bank of America to avoid going under. There were apparently about seven hundred senior staff recipients. The total has been estimated at US$3.6 billion - during a quarter when the company lost over US$15 billion. Many of these recipients were the same staff that took the risk that pretty well brought down the company. That is just sickening.

But where was the value in what these financial types were doing? Who was paying the fees on all this complex investing activity? Wasn't it the little guy or gal who invested his or her money in the market, or took out a mortgage on their home?

Didn't that million-dollar bonus come out of the pocket of the person who worked hard every day at a job making $20 per hour? The guy sweating it out on the assembly line? The girl running her own business selling clothing? The person cutting lawns and plowing driveways for a living?

It doesn't make a lot of sense to me. Eventually, when greed drives a sufficient number of people to want to make more and more money each and every year off the little guy or gal, you end up breaking the little guy or gal's back. And that is what has happened in the U.S.

The person who had a house worth, say, $200,000, and mortgaged it to the hilt to spend and try to invest, has seen the value of the home plunge. Many still owe more than the house is worth even six years later. If they had a retirement fund, it too has plunged in value and for many, has not even reached pre-crash levels. And now, their jobs are at risk. It's a perfect storm – a big one.

Most Canadians are in much better shape than many Americans. We are a more conservative nation and the "get rich at all costs" mantra is not so deeply ingrained in our genes. Having said that, we still have problems: will the stock market keep growing as it has since the bottom of the crash in early 2009? Will our housing market keep up the pace, or are we in for a shock like our American friends? What about jobs – why are our young having such a hard time finding jobs and will that continue?

It's going to be a tough journey but there is hope. Let's build that hope on a solid foundation.

Let's forget the stock market. Don't buy another mutual fund. Sleep at night knowing your investments will NEVER decline.

Instead, live life without reading about stock market gyrations, the criminal CEOs that reduced their company to a shell of its former self in the quest for personal riches, or the scam artist who sold out his clients with a get-rich-quick scheme.

WHO WANTS TO BE RICH?

You want to be rich, right? Get all the cool toys whenever you want. Take five vacations a year. Own a luxury car. But what does it take to get rich? It often takes risk.

Are you willing to literally risk everything to get rich? Would you risk your house, the ability to pay for your kids' education, your ability to buy food when you retire? Well, that is what you are essentially doing if you put all your eggs in the stock market basket.

Those that wanted to get rich easily and borrowed to invest in the stock market have been particularly hard-hit. There was even a book out there encouraging this scheme. It told people how they could "make their mortgage tax deductible." The idea was that every time you made a mortgage payment, you would immediately take the principal repayment portion and borrow that amount to invest in mutual funds. Essentially you would never pay down your mortgage. The value of your house would eventually equal the amount you put into the mutual funds.

Investment dealers loved this idea. The main proponent of this scheme was able to charge speaker fees of thousands of dollars to help convince the unwary to sign up and begin flowing money each and every week to the investment advisors.

I feel very sorry for those people now. They have put the biggest asset they own – their house – at risk and are stuck with expensive, poorly performing mutual funds and a ton of debt.

This scheme violates another point of The Antidote – buy your house and pay it off before you retire.

If you want to take a risk in an attempt to get rich, don't do it with your house or the funds you'll need to raise your kids or eat when you no longer work – just buy a lottery ticket. I'm serious. You may get rich but if not, all you've lost is a few bucks, not your home or your future.

WHY YOU DON'T NEED STOCKS

They sell the stock market as a great way to get wealthy. How else can you double or triple your money without any effort on your part? The problem is that it is risky. You are just as likely to end up losing your money. Think about the people who picked the wrong companies in the past and lost everything. Those who trusted Enron, WorldCom, Nortel, Lehman Brothers, Washington Mutual, and their ilk.

Even if you only invest in solid companies with established earnings, excellent products and revolutionary new ideas, you could lose big time. Take Apple Computers (Nasdaq: AAPL), for example. They have produced game-changing products like the iPod, iPhone, iPad, in addition to award-winning computers like the MacBook Pro and Air notebook and the iMac - all incredible products that consumers want.

What happened to their share price during 2007 to 2009? Figure 2.1 shows their month-end share price during that period:

FIGURE 2.1 Apple's Month-end Share Price from 2007 to 2009

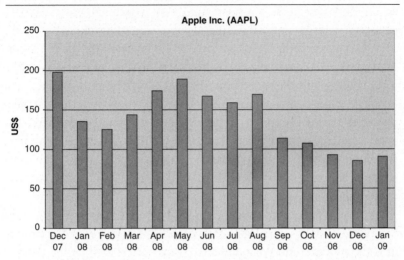

Apple's stock price peaked on December 28, 2007 at US$199.83. On January 9, 2009 it closed at US$90.58. That's a decline of US$109.25 or 55%. And that was during a period where they were making good money.

For the twelve months ended September 30, 2007, its revenues were US$24.006 billion and its net income was US$3.496 billion. The year ended September 30, 2008 saw revenues increase to US$32.479 billion and net income grow to US$4.834 billion. That was a 35% increase in revenue and a 38% increase in net income. The fact that Apple's stock price dropped so much defies logic. But that's the point – the stock market is not very logical. It's driven by emotion and feelings, not common sense.

WHY YOU DON'T NEED MUTUAL FUNDS - RISK

Mutual funds were invented to allow the individual investor access to a diversified portfolio of investments that is managed by a professional money manager. They therefore avoid the potential disaster associated with picking the wrong individual company.

OK, so your risk is reduced because with a mutual fund you'll own a number of different companies. But there are still significant other risks. I am looking at a prospectus for a mutual fund that I was personally invested in. It is a bond fund with a well-known investment company whose name you would recognize in an instant.

Current regulations require these companies to disclose the different types of risks an investor faces when they make purchases. The prospectus begins the section on risk by stating that mutual funds own different types of investments depending on their investment objectives and that the value of the investments a mutual fund owns will vary from day to day because of changes in interest rates and economic conditions, as well as market and company news. The result is that the value of any mutual fund's units may go up or down by the time you redeem them.

It further goes on to state that the full amount of any investment in their mutual funds is not guaranteed and that "unlike bank accounts or GICs, mutual fund units and shares are not covered by the Canada Deposit Insurance Corporation (CDIC) or any other government deposit insurer."

Talk about risk! If your mutual fund company happens to go under, don't bother calling the CDIC - they can't help.

The prospectus also indicates that their mutual funds may invest in different classes of securities, including bonds, equities and cash, depending on the specific fund's objectives. For example, a fund with an objective of long-term capital gain will invest mostly in equities, whereas a fund whose aim is to preserve capital will invest mostly in bonds and money market securities.

As a result, different mutual funds will carry different types of risks depending on the securities they own. The following is a long list of the eighteen types of risk you expose yourself to, depending on the specific mutual funds you invest in.

Mutual Fund Risks

WARNING: The following list is long and boring, but if you own mutual funds you have to understand each and every one of them!

1. **Credit Risk.** This is the risk that a company that issues a bond or other fixed-income security won't be able to repay the principal or interest when it comes due. Generally, you'll put yourself at less risk if the issuer has a high credit rating from

an independent credit rating agency. And, the prices of securities with higher ratings tend to be less volatile than those with lower ratings.

2. **Derivative Risk.** Some funds have the leeway to use derivatives – in essence, contracts that gamble on the future prices of assets – often using them in an attempt to avoid risk. The fund's description will tell you if it does. So it may seem odd that derivatives themselves have their own kinds of risk, including that the use of derivatives for hedging may not be effective, that some derivatives may limit a fund's potential for gains and not just losses, and that you, Joe Investor, may have to pay for the cost of entering and maintaining derivative contracts through reductions in the fund's total return. And that's just for starters.

3. **Emerging Markets Risk.** Emerging markets … sounds alluring, doesn't it? But the potential for earning a strong return from developing economies is offset by their smaller securities markets, which make it more difficult to sell securities to take profits or avoid losses; their lower regulation standards; their political instability and possible corruption; and the difficulty of determining the true value of a company.

4. **Equity Risk.** Very simply, if a basket of stocks or shares rises in market value, then the funds that invest in it rise as well. So, strong economy begets positive company outlook begets generally rising share prices. And weak economy begets lacklustre or negative company outlook begets generally failing share prices. And there's no crystal ball telling us which way the economy is headed.

5. **Foreign Currency Risk.** The value of securities that are issued in foreign currencies and that earn income in foreign funds is affected by the value of the Canadian dollar relative to those currencies. For example, if the value of the foreign currency declined relative to the Canadian dollar, so too would the value of the foreign securities.

6. **Foreign Equity Risk.** Investments across the border, any border, are risky because of possible political or social instability, lack of information about foreign companies, and

possibly lower standards of government supervision and regulation than in Canada. And, if the fund runs into trouble, it may have difficulty pursuing legal action in jurisdictions outside Canada.

7. **Interest Rate Risk.** The interest rate on a bond is set when it's issued. If interest rates fall, the price of an existing bond will rise because it's paying a higher rate than newer bonds and is therefore more valuable. Conversely, if interest rates rise, the value of an existing bond and any fund holding such bonds will fall. Funds that include convertible securities also carry interest rate risk.

8. **Large Investor Risk.** Large investors, such as financial institutions, may redeem or purchase securities of a fund. Their actions may be substantial enough to force the portfolio manager to change significantly the composition of the portfolio or to buy or sell investments at unfavourable prices, which can negatively affect return.

9. **Liquidity Risk.** Securities with a limited trading market have liquidity risk. Because they're difficult to sell, if supply outweighs demand for them they may trade at an amount lower than their value. To mitigate this risk, many set a limit for "illiquid securities."

10. **Low-Rated Security Risk.** Some companies offer a higher rate of return because they carry a higher risk. They may have a credit rating below investment grade or perhaps be unrated. These investments may be hard to value because market quotations aren't available and they may be less liquid than higher-grade investments. They have the potential for large gains or losses.

11. **Regulatory Risk.** Industries such as health care and telecommunications are heavily regulated and may receive government funding. Changes in government policy such as deregulation or reduced government funding may substantially affect companies in these sectors, so funds that buy these investments may rise and fall substantially.

12. **Repurchase/Reverse Repurchase Agreements Risk.** A repurchase agreement involves selling a security at one price

and simultaneously agreeing to buy it back at a lower price. A reverse repurchase agreement involves buying a security at one price and simultaneously agreeing to sell it back at a higher price. This creates lots of risks. Funds then jump through hoops to reduce those risks, by holding offsetting collateral, and putting in place a series of conditions for these transactions.

13. **RSP Fund Risk.** RSP funds use forward contracts, debt-like securities and other specified derivatives as part of their investment strategy, which involves some specific risks in addition to the general risks of derivatives themselves. For one thing, if the underlying fund to an RSP fund runs into trouble and suspends redemptions, the corresponding RSP fund will be unable to value part of its portfolio or redeem units. Then what? And, there's the cost of the derivatives, which is borne by the RSP fund itself and eats into the returns of the RSP fund, and potential problems surrounding counterparties. Starting to feel tense yet?

14. **Securities Lending Risk.** Some funds can lend a portion of their portfolio securities to a qualified borrower or borrowers who have posted collateral for a fee and a set period of time. These funds run the risk that a borrower may not fulfill its obligations, leaving the fund holding collateral worth less than the securities it has lent, and resulting in a loss to the fund. To limit this risk, a cap is set on how much and what type of collateral can be held, on how much the fund can lend through such transactions, and on how much exposure it can have to any one borrower.

15. **Series Risk.** Your fund may have several series of units, each with its own fees and expenses, which are tracked separately from other series. If one series can't pay its portion of expenses based on its proportionate share of the fund assets, another series may have to help out. If your fund is the one helping out its down-on-luck brother, your investment return is probably going to suffer.

16. **Smaller Company Risk.** The stock price of smaller companies is often more volatile than that of larger, more established

companies. This is because they may be developing new products that haven't been tested in the marketplace, their existing products quickly become obsolete, they usually have limited access to funding, and may suffer from inexperienced management, not to mention that they usually trade in smaller volumes and less frequently than larger company shares so any share purchase or sale has a greater impact on their share price.

17. **Tax Class Fund Risk.** While assets and liabilities of each Tax Class Fund are tracked separately, the investment company, Tax Class Corp., as a whole is responsible for all of the financial obligations of the Tax Class Funds combined. If a Tax Class Fund cannot pay its expenses using its proportionate share of the assets, the investment company, Tax Class Corp., may have to pay those expenses out of the other Tax Class Funds' assets, which could lower the investment return of those other Tax Class Funds. As well, the tax consequences of an investment in a Tax Class Fund will depend in part on the tax position of the investment company, Tax Class Corp., as a whole and will differ from an investment in a mutual fund that is not part of a multi-class structure.

18. **Underlying Fund Risk.** The investment company and unaffiliated third parties may offer investment products that use a "fund on fund" structure whereby a "top fund" invests all or a significant portion of its assets in a "bottom" or "underlying fund." Depending on the size of the investment being made by a top fund in an underlying fund and the timing of the redemption of this investment, an underlying fund could be forced to alter significantly its portfolio assets to accommodate a large redemption order, having a negative impact on the performance of the underlying fund.

That's a lot of risk isn't it? Well, if you own mutual funds, you need to be aware of and understand the ins and outs of every one of these different types of risks.

THOSE DARN MUTUAL FUND FEES!

OK, We've established that mutual funds are risky and have learned the hard way that they can fall significantly and that can happen quickly. But there is another huge reason you don't need mutual funds: excessive, draining and hidden fees.

Oh, thank you – the mutual fund prospectus I'm looking at has a whole section titled "Fees and Expenses." Let's have a look, shall we?

It starts off by noting that some of the fees are paid directly by you and that others are "payable by the funds or portfolios, which will indirectly reduce the value of your investment in the fund or portfolio." In other words, some you'll see taken directly out of your investment account and some will be taken out of the pool of money you have contributed to.

Let's start with the section on fees and expenses payable directly by you:

1. Fees and Expenses Payable Directly by You
Sales Charges

Most mutual fund companies divide their offerings into different "series" of units and the one we have been talking about is no exception. In this case they are either "front load" or "rear load."

Front-Load Option

You pay up to 6% of the purchase price, as negotiated between you and your dealer.

Interesting observation: many of the fees your investment advisor charges you are negotiable. Did you know that?

Rear-Load (Deferred Sales Charge) Option

In all likelihood, you have never purchased a front-load type fund. The usual line from the salespeople is "Why would you? You'd like all your money working for you, wouldn't you?"

So they convince you that a rear-load, or deferred sales charge (DSC), option is the best.

Under this option, you pay a redemption fee if you redeem your units within a certain number of years of buying them – up to six years, in this company's case. Here's the scale of fees:

- 6.0% in the first year after purchase
- 5.5% in the second year
- 5.0% in the third year
- 4.5% in the fourth year
- 4.0% in the fifth year
- 3.0% in the sixth year
- nil after six years

The redemption fee may be based on the original cost of the units or the market value when you cash them in. In this company's case, it's the original cost. In declining stock markets this can really add insult to injury. Say you purchased $10,000 of the DSC series of the equity fund before the market crash of 2008. Your $10,000 tanked to $6,000 and you'd like to get out. The cost to sell and realize the $4,000 loss before it gets worse? It's 6% of $10,000, or $600. Ouch.

Switch fees
It may cost you up to 2% as negotiated between you and your dealer to change funds.

Short-Term Trading Fees
You'll pay up to 2% if you request to switch out of any fund within two weeks of an earlier switch request, switch more than twice within a 90-day period or "appear to follow a market timing pattern that may adversely affect a fund or portfolio."

Registered Plan Fees Payable to the Trustee
Such fees include semi-annual trustee fees for Registered Education Savings Plans (RESPs; $7.50 in this case), other registered plans (0.20% of account value, minimum $7.50, maximum $25) and RSP redemption fees ($15 per redemption plus any deferred sales charge).

Other fees
These fees include bank costs for wiring redemption proceeds to your account.

2. Fees and Expenses Payable by the Fund or Portfolio

Management Fees

Management fees are paid by the mutual funds to the investment manager for investment management and general administrative services. A portion of the management fees are sales commissions and trail fees paid to dealers who bring in the clients' money.

The prospectus I am looking at states that they paid dealers 56% of the total management fees they earned on all funds and portfolios and that "this amount included sales commissions and trail fees as well as our support of their promotional activities." Do you know what that means? It means current investors are paying so the mutual fund managers can attract more clients. That's a sweet deal – for them.

Just what are "trail fees?" They're fees, usually ranging from 0.5% to 1.0% per year, that are paid to your dealer as long as you own the funds. This is for the ongoing advice they are supposed to be providing you. Are you getting your money's worth? In many cases the answer is no. Sometimes, advisors don't even return your phone calls!

And here's another interesting tidbit: Even with a DSC mutual fund where you, as the investor, do not pay a front-load fee, this particular company pays the dealer a sales commission of 5% of the amount you invested, through the management expenses. But you'll still be subject to the redemption fee if you cash out within six years. Talk about having your cake and eating it too!

And another one: They may reduce the management expenses for certain investors. Their decision depends on the size and nature of the investment. In other words, the big guys like pension funds, insurers and other institutional investors get a discount on fees. You, small fry, don't.

Operating Expenses

Mutual funds are like large companies. They have infrastructures that have to be maintained and that costs money. Here is a list of the operating expenses that the funds have to pay:

- legal
- audit

- custodial
- registrar and transfer agent fees
- bank fees and expenses
- cost of preparing financial statements, prospectuses and other reports
- other administrative expenses
- taxes

The Management Expense Ratio (MER)

You may be familiar with the term "Management Expense Ratio" (MER), as it is often discussed in the media when it comes to the cost of owning mutual funds. The MER shows how much a fund paid in management fees and operating expenses (including goods and services tax and harmonized sales tax) during a year. It is expressed as an annualized percentage of the daily average net assets during the year.

Generally, the MER for equity based mutual funds is higher than for fixed-income or bond funds because choosing and monitoring hundreds of different companies' shares is more labour-intensive than choosing a series of fixed-income securities.

If you invest in mutual funds, you should know what the MER is for each and every one. In Canada, these fees are among the highest in the world, In fact, in their 2013 Global Fund Investor Experience Report, Morningstar states that Canada actually does have the highest annual expense ratios for equity funds in the world at 2.42%.

Ever wonder why it seems you never manage to get ahead with Canadian equity mutual funds, even when the stock market is heading the right way? Fees, fees and more fees!

The Puke Point

The Puke Point is that point in an investors life when it all just becomes too much. You can't help but regurgitate every one of your remaining stocks and mutual funds and resolve never to own another one. (No I didn't invent that term but I wish I did!).

But there is a problem when it comes to getting rid of your mutual funds: it could cost you a huge amount of money. The brilliance of the creators of mutual funds now becomes even more evident.

Not only have they guaranteed their constant annual income through visible and hidden fees even when your investment value goes down, they make it very costly for you to leave.

Let's look at a simple example. I have used a common Canadian equity mutual fund purchased on January 1, 2008 and sold on December 31, 2008. It is an actual DSC fund of the investment company whose prospectus I have been talking about.

The Net Asset Value (NAV) per unit on January 1, 2008 was $69.93. Let's say we had $10,000 and we therefore bought 143 units (143 units × $69.93 each = $10,000). Since this is a DSC fund, the full $10,000 was invested and showed on our investment statement in January.

As we know, our investment advisor got his sales commission of 5% of $10,000. He got $500 out of the pot of money the mutual fund had from all investors like us. That fee is reflected in the annual return of the mutual fund, which affects the ending value of the mutual fund.

The NAV of this mutual fund actually rose to $76 in May of 2008, but the value on December 31, 2008 was only $49.66. The value of our investment on December 31, 2008 was therefore $7,101.38 (143 units × $49.66 each). In that one year we lost $2,898.62 or 29% of our money.

But at this point it's an unrealized loss. We could hold on and hope things get better. But let's say we've had enough and want to limit our losses to 29%. What is the cost to redeem our units? Well, it's that ugly DCS fee of 6.0% in the first year after purchase. And it's on the original value of the investment −$10,000 in this case.

Kiss goodbye $600.

The amount of money we'll get out is only $6,501.38. That's the $7,101.38 our investment value had declined to, less the $600 DSC fee.

Our total loss was $3,498.62 – 35% of our original investment.

How to Get Rid of Your "Dog" Funds

The irony of getting to a 100% safe investment strategy is that getting out of the losing mutual funds you have accumulated over the years is the hardest part because it is so costly.

My advice would be not to overreact and dump them all at once. It's probably best to take an organized approach to getting to safety. It's also not a good idea to just dump your investment advisor at this stage. You'll need him or her to help make the changes you'll want to make.

Step #1: The 10% Peel

The first step is to realize that you are allowed to redeem up to 10% of the units of a mutual fund in each calendar year without paying a redemption fee. Start by instructing your advisor to do this for each of the funds you'd like to get rid of. It's not quick, but at least it's a start.

Step #2: What'll it Cost Me to Get Out?

The second step is to ask your advisor to get the following information for each of the mutual funds you own:

- the DSC redemption charge you would pay to cash in the fund as of a certain date
- the date the fund will be "DSC free" or cashable with no redemption fee

Once you've assembled all the information you'll have a decision to make on each fund.

You may be lucky enough to have some funds that you have held long enough that there will be no DSC fee. In other cases, the fee may be small enough that you'd be willing to take the hit and pay the fee just to get rid of the fund.

In other cases, you may think it best to hold on for another year or two in the hopes that the market comes back. In this case, make sure that you have confidence in the fund manager who will be making the important decisions in the fund over whatever period you are going to hold on to it for.

The key recommendation is to be patient. It took years to get into the mess you are in. It's best not to try and get out in one day.

A Word about Labour-Sponsored Investment Funds

Labour-Sponsored Investment Funds (LSIFs) were created to give a special tax break to people willing to invest in start-up Canadian businesses through special mutual funds. The break is given because there is a high risk that many of the start-ups won't survive. Some of the investments will have to be written off, which will affect the funds' rates of return.

It's the possibility of a star company emerging that makes them more attractive. For example, Research in Motion, maker of the Black-Berry, was originally funded by an LSIF.

The problem is that the majority of these investment companies have a short history and most are not publicly traded. It is therefore difficult to value them. Most LSIFs also have high MERs – in many cases over 4%.

LSIFs were very popular in the 1990s because of generous federal and provincial tax breaks and some initial good returns. The tax breaks have been scaled back in recent years, however, and the returns of these funds has been unimpressive – negative in many cases.

Most people (me included) originally got into LSIFs for the tax breaks. The federal government used to offer a 20% tax credit (that has been reduced to 15%) on the first $5,000 invested in an LSIF. Most provinces offered an additional 15% credit. This added up to quite the tax break, especially for LSIFs held in an RRSP account. For example, if you were in the 40% marginal tax bracket you'd get a $2,000 income tax refund on the $5,000 RRSP contribution, a $750 tax credit from the federal government and $750 from the provincial one. Your $5,000 contribution cost you only $1,500 ($5,000 - $2,000 - $750 -$750).

The catch is that you have to hold onto the investments for eight years (five years before 1996); otherwise, you'll have to pay those juicy tax credits back.

If you own some LSIFs, find out what date you'll be free from paying back the tax credits. And before you consider buying another one, check that your province or territory still gives a tax credit. Ontario, for example, no longer does.

WE WON'T GET FOOLED AGAIN

OK, let's begin the journey to a safe, comfortable retirement. We've agreed to swear off the stock market and mutual funds and never blindly trust another person, be it a stranger, a relative or a friend, to handle our hard-earned savings. Well what *do* we put our money in?

We only put it in fixed-income products that can NEVER decline in value. That basically means GICs (guaranteed investment certificates), term deposits or high-income savings accounts. We also don't know how financially strong all the financial institutions are, so we have to make sure they are all 100% guaranteed by the federal government. That means we need to find out all there is to know about the Canada Deposit Insurance Corporation (CDIC).

The Canada Deposit Insurance Corporation

We are going to invest only in things that are guaranteed never to lose their value but we also want to make sure they are insured if the issuer goes bust.

In Canada, the CDIC was created by parliament in 1967 as a federal Crown corporation. The CDIC insures Canadians' savings should their bank, or other CDIC member institution, fail or go bankrupt. It is not a bank or an insurance company.

You don't need to sign up for the insurance and you don't need to pay for it, either. The CDIC is funded by fees from its member institutions.

While banks in Canada seldom fail, they can and do. Take a guess how many Canadian institutions have failed and had to be bailed out by the CDIC. My guess was a dozen. The real number? 43.

Yes, that's right, since the CDIC was created in 1967, 43 institutions have failed. Here's the list posted at http://www.cdic .ca/WhereInsured/FailureHistory/Pages/default.aspx, as shown in Table 2.3. Hopefully you don't recognize any.

What the CDIC Covers

The CDIC only insures certain types of investments as follows:

- savings and chequing accounts
- GICs and other term deposits that mature in five years or less
- money orders, certified cheques, travellers' cheques and bank drafts issued by CDIC members
- accounts that hold realty taxes on mortgaged properties

What the CDIC Doesn't Cover

It does not insure these:

- mutual funds and stocks
- GICs and other term deposits that mature in more than five years
- U.S. dollar or other foreign currency deposits

TABLE 2.3   History of Member Institution Failures

CDIC Member Institution	Year of Failure
Commonwealth Trust Company	1970
Security Trust Company Limited	1972
Astra Trust Company	1980
District Trust Company	1982
AMIC Mortgage Investment Corporation	1983
Crown Trust Company	1983
Fidelity Trust Company	1983
Greymac Mortgage Corporation	1983
Greymac Trust Company	1983
Seaway Mortgage Corporation	1983
Seaway Trust Company	1983
Northguard Mortgage Corporation	1984
CCB Mortgage Investment Corporation	1985
Canadian Commercial Bank	1985
Continental Trust Company	1985
London Loan Limited	1985
Northland Bank	1985
Pioneer Trust Company	1985
Western Capital Trust Company	1985
Bank of British Columbia	1986
Bank of British Columbia Mortgage Corporation	1986
Columbia Trust Company	1986
North West Trust Company	1987
Principal Savings & Trust Company	1987
Financial Trust Company	1988
Settlers Savings and Mortgage Corporation	1990
Bank of Credit and Commerce Canada	1991
Saskatchewan Trust Company	1991
Standard Loan Company	1991
Standard Trust Company	1991
Shoppers Trust Company	1992

(*continued overleaf*)

TABLE 2.3 *(continued)*

CDIC Member Institution	Year of Failure
Central Guaranty Mortgage Corporation	1992
Central Guaranty Trust Company	1992
First City Trust Company	1992
First City Mortgage Company	1992
Dominion Trust Company	1993
Prenor Trust Company of Canada	1993
Confederation Trust Company	1994
Monarch Trust Company	1994
Income Trust Company	1995
North American Trust Company	1995
NAL Mortgage Company	1995
Security Home Mortgage Corporation	1996

Source: CDIC www.cdic.ca

- principal-protected notes issued by corporations, including banks or other CDIC members
- bonds, notes and debentures issued by governments or corporations, including banks and other CDIC members (except for debentures issued to evidence deposits by member institutions, other than banks)

It should be noted that these rules apply even if your investments are in a Registered Retirement Savings Plan (RRSP), Registered Retirement Income Fund (RRIF) or Tax Free Savings Accounts (TFSA). For example, if your RRSP is with a CDIC member institution but all it holds is mutual funds, you are not insured. That includes money market mutual funds.

Certain debentures issued by CDIC member institutions other than banks are the equivalent of a certificate for a term deposit. These debentures are eligible for deposit insurance. But a debenture issued by a bank, other corporation or government is a debt security and is therefore not covered by deposit insurance because it is not the equivalent of a certificate for a term deposit.

The CDIC does not cover losses due to fraud, theft or scams.

The CDIC Can Cover More Than $100,000

Here's some good news: the CDIC insures up to $100,000 in up to seven categories at one institution. Here's the list of savings you can hold:

1. **In one name.** This can be personal, business or other organization.
2. **Joint deposits.** For example married couples or business partners.
3. **Trust account.** An account set up by a trustee for a beneficiary (i.e. a grandmother setting up a savings account for a grandchild to use later).
4. **An RRSP.** A Registered Retirement Savings Account.
5. **A RRIF.** A Registered Retirement Income Fund.
6. **TFSA.** A Tax-Free Savings Account.
7. **A Realty Tax account.** Deposits made towards realty taxes on mortgaged properties.

So if you had $100,000 in one of each of these accounts at one CDIC member institution, fully $700,000 would be covered by the CDIC.

List of CDIC Members

Make sure your financial institution is a member of the CDIC by checking their website (www.cdic.ca). Here is the current list of members as of July 2014:

Amex Bank of Canada
B2B Bank
B2B Trustco
Bank of China (Canada)
Bank of Montreal
Bank of Montreal Mortgage
  Corporation
Bank of Nova Scotia (The)
Bank West
BMO Trust Company
Bridgewater Bank
Canada Trust Company (The)
Canadian Imperial Bank of
  Commerce

Canadian Tire Bank
Canadian Western Bank
Canadian Western Trust Company
CFF Bank
CIBC Mellon Trust Company
CIBC Mortgages Inc.
CIBC Trust Corporation
Citibank Canada
Citizens Bank of Canada
Community Trust Company
Computershare Trust Company of
  Canada
Concentra Financial Services
  Association

Concentra Trust
CS Alterna Bank
CTBC Bank Corp. (Canada)
Desjardins Trust Inc.
DirectCash Bank
Effort Trust Company (The)
Equitable Bank
Equity Financial Trust Company
First Nations Bank of Canada
General Bank of Canada
Habib Canadian Bank
Hollis Canadian Bank
Home Trust Company
HomEquity Bank
HSBC Bank Canada
HSBC Mortgage Corporation (Canada)
HSBC Trust Company (Canada)
ICICI Bank Canada
Industrial Alliance Trust Inc.
Industrial and Commercial Bank of China (Canada)
Investors Group Trust Co. Ltd.
Korea Exchange Bank of Canada
Laurentian Bank of Canada
Laurentian Trust of Canada Inc.
LBC Trust
League Savings and Mortgage Company

Manulife Bank of Canada
Manulife Trust Company
MCAN Mortgage Corporation
Mega International Commercial Bank (Canada)
Montreal Trust Company of Canada
Natcan Trust Company
National Bank of Canada
National Bank Trust Inc.
National Trust Company
Pacific & Western Bank of Canada
Peace Hills Trust Company
Peoples Trust Company
President's Choice Bank
RBC Investor Services Trust
Royal Bank Mortgage Corporation
Royal Bank of Canada
Royal Trust Company (The)
Royal Trust Corporation of Canada
Scotia Mortgage Corporation
Shinhan Bank Canada
State Bank of India (Canada)
Sun Life Financial Trust Inc.
Tangerine Bank
TD Mortgage Corporation
TD Pacific Mortgage Corporation
Toronto-Dominion Bank (The)
UBS Bank (Canada)
Valiant Trust Company

The Advantages of GICs

There are many advantages to GICs. Here are a few of them.

Easy to Understand

What you see is what you get. Your investment statement will show what the GIC was purchased for, what the term is (i.e. one-year, five-year) and what the annual interest rate is. You'll know exactly what it will be worth at any point in time going forward. Oh, and it won't ever be worth less than you paid for it because the principal is guaranteed at maturity.

No Fees

Even if you buy a GIC through an investment advisor, any fees that he or she might earn for placing the GIC with a financial institution won't (or shouldn't!) come from the interest earned by the GIC. In other words you should pay no up-front fee to invest in them and even if the advisor gets paid a fee, it does not come out of your return. This is unlike mutual funds, where fees can be eating away at your investment through the management expenses of the mutual fund itself – fees that you don't really see.

Flexible

It used to be that you had to lock in your funds for a fixed period of time and if you cashed early for any reason you would pay a large penalty – often any interest you had earned to date. Now there are many types and terms of cashable GICs.

Insured

As we have seen, GICs are insured by the CDIC so that if the institution where you hold your GIC (whether inside or outside an RRSP) goes under, you'll get your money back. This is not the case with mutual funds – even money-market ones – as they are not covered by CDIC insurance.

Why They Try to Make Even GICs Complicated

Just like anything else when it comes to investments, even GICs can get confusing. There are a couple of advantages to making investment products as complicated and confusing as possible. They are advantages if you are a seller, though. To you as a buyer, complication is your enemy.

The first advantage is that fees are much easier to extract when it comes to complicated products. For example, do you really understand how equity mutual funds work? How about income trusts? They are extremely complex, risky vehicles that make it virtually impossible to figure out how much the advisors and sponsors get paid. But be assured, they do get paid, even if your investment is devastated by performance losses.

The second advantage to complexity is that it makes it difficult for you to figure out how well the investment is doing. You may have heard something like this: "It's too complicated to figure out and even if we could, you probably wouldn't understand."

Are you kidding me? They want to put us in a product that is so complicated that they, the sellers, can't even figure out the personal rate of return? Don't believe it. They know exactly how well it's doing. They're just worried that if you knew, you'd take your money elsewhere - somewhere you could be assured you weren't getting taken.

That's why they invent things like market-linked and escalating rate GICs.

How and Why They Bash GICs

I am tired of seeing the following arguments against GICs:

> "Sure GICs are safe, but have you ever considered the tax and inflation affects? You may even be losing money! If your GIC is earning 2.5% a year, you'll pay tax on the interest earned and if you are in the 40% income tax bracket, that 2.5% a year means you'll only earn 1.5% after paying 1.0% (2.5% × 0.40% tax) in taxes. Since inflation is around 1.5%, your real rate of return is actually zero!"

This argument is then usually followed by the advice to invest in the stock market. Hopefully you did not read such an article before the fall of 2008. Here is why the arguments don't make sense to me.

First of all, for investments outside tax sheltered vehicles like RRSPs, RRIFs and Tax-Free Savings Accounts (TFSAs), it is correct that interest income from a GIC is taxed as normal income is, at 100%. Capital gains from the sale of stocks and mutual funds are taxed at only 50% of the gain. That's why I recommend that you hold GICs in RRSPs, RRIFs, and TFSAs. In this way, you retain the full 2.5% rate of return, at least until you withdraw the funds in the case of RRSPs and RRIFs.

The second argument about inflation is a red herring. What does inflation have to do with investment returns? Inflation surely does have a significant effect on the price of the things you buy, but even if inflation is rising, is that a good reason to remove the safety net of the GIC principal guarantee and risk losing your money in the stock market?

In other words, assume you are retired and on a fixed income and your property taxes rose 5% last year to $4,200 from $4,000, an increase of $200. Does the fact that your conservative retirement nest-egg RRIF only went up from $200,000 to $205,000, an increase of 2.5% before inflation, bother you?

I'll tell you what would bother me. If my $200,000 RRIF that was 50% invested in the stock market dove to $157,500. That would be the case if the $100,000 in the Canadian stock market lost $45,000 (45%) and declined to $55,000, while the other $100,000 in GICs went up to $102,500 (a 2.5% increase) for a total value of $157,500 ($55,000 plus $102,500).

What would you do if you sold the stock market for a living? You'd probably dream up other reasons to bash GICs too. But you don't sell the stock market for a living, do you? Well then, if you want to get ahead, don't listen to the people who do, and avoid potential personal financial disasters.

The Laddered GIC

Once you do start investing, consider putting your money in a sure thing that can't lose: GIC's, term deposits or high interest savings accounts. Resolve not to pay another dime to the investment "advisors" that get rich off you behind the scenes with hidden fees and commissions while putting your retirement at risk.

A word of warning: unfortunately you can't simply switch your mutual funds for GICs even within the same RRSP with the same company. You'll still be subject to all the DSC and other fees to get out. That's because switching will mean your investment advisor and his company won't be able to soak you for huge fees anymore. They will probably try to dissuade you from switching at all costs. How are they going to be able to afford to put that second story on the cottage on Lake Muskoka if you switch!?

Let's delve into the "laddered GIC" strategy of investing in short-, medium- and long-term savings vehicles to make sure cash is available when needed and to increase your overall returns.

Remember, the CDIC only covers GICs and term deposits that mature in five years or less so five years is the longest we can buy.

Here is how the strategy works:

- **Step 1.** Divide whatever amount you have by five.
- **Step 2.** Invest 20% (one-fifth) in each of a one-, two-, three-, four- and five-year GIC.
- **Step 3**. Each year that any of the GICs mature, reinvest the proceeds in a five-year GIC at the prevailing rate.

Let's have a look at how the strategy would have worked over the last ten years starting in 2004.

According to the Bank of Canada (http://www.bankofcanada.ca/rates/interest-rates/canadian-interest-rates/), from 2004 to 2014, the average GIC rates were as follows, shown in Table 2.4:

TABLE 2.4   Average GIC Rates from 2004 to 2014

	2004	2005	2006	2007	2008	2009	2010	2011	2012	2013	2014
One-Year	1.19%	1.53%	2.78%	2.98%	2.14%	0.40%	0.62%	1.01%	0.95%	0.78%	0.95%
Three-Year	2.23%	2.15%	2.99%	3.14%	2.69%	1.52%	1.41%	1.35%	1.18%	1.24%	1.13%
Five-Year	2.92%	2.71%	3.16%	3.31%	3.05%	1.95%	1.97%	1.87%	1.65%	1.63%	1.85%

Source: Bank of Canada *www.bankofcanada.ca*

Let's look at the results of the laddered GIC strategy used for the ten-year period 2004 to 2014. Have a look at the chart in Figure 2.2.

Have a look at Strategy 1: Rolling over at consistent term in the chart. It shows that over the ten-year period from 2004 to 2014 if we had simply invested in 100% government-guaranteed GICs and rolled the one-, two-, three-, four- and five-year GICs over at the same term each time they came due, our original $50,000 would have grown to a value of $61,510.59. That is an average annual rate of return of 2.09%.

But there is an easy way to increase your returns. You can simply apply the laddered GIC strategy to benefit from the higher longer-term rates.

Look at Strategy 2: Rolling over to five-year at the bottom of the chart. It shows that the higher five-year rates would grow the original $50,000 to $64,066.66. That is $2,556.07 better than Strategy 1 and represents an average annual rate of return of 2.51% a year.

FIGURE 2.2   GIC strategy used for the period 2004 to 2014

GIC Laddered 2004 - 2014

Initial investment:	$50,000.00
Start Date:	June 1, 2004
End Date:	June 1, 2014

	2004	2005	2006	2007	2008	2009	2010	2011	2012	2013	2014
One-Year	1.19	1.53	2.78	2.98	2.14	0.40	0.62	1.01	0.95	0.78	0.95
Two-Year	1.71	1.84	2.89	3.06	2.42	0.96	1.02	1.18	1.07	1.01	1.04
Three-Year	2.23	2.15	2.99	3.14	2.69	1.52	1.41	1.35	1.18	1.24	1.13
Four-Year	2.58	2.43	3.08	3.23	2.87	1.74	1.69	1.61	1.42	1.44	1.49
Five-Year	2.92	2.71	3.16	3.31	3.05	1.95	1.97	1.87	1.65	1.63	1.85

Strategy 1: Rolling over at consistent term

#	2004	2005	2006	2007	2008	2009	2010	2011	2012	2013	2014	
1	$10,000.00	$10,119.00	$10,273.82	$10,559.43	$10,874.10	$11,106.81	$11,151.24	$11,220.37	$11,333.70	$11,441.37		$11,530.61
2	$10,000.00		$10,344.92		$10,950.44		$11,485.73		$11,720.07			$11,971.04
3	$10,000.00			$10,684.03			$11,671.33			$12,211.67		$12,363.10
4	$10,000.00				$11,070.47				$12,569.14			$12,927.37
5	$10,000.00					$11,547.79						$12,718.47
	$50,000.00											**$61,510.59**

Strategy 2: Rolling over to five-year

#	2004	2005	2006	2007	2008	2009	2010	2011	2012	2013	2014	
1	$10,000.00	$10,119.00					$11,566.48					$12,505.21
2	$10,000.00		$10,344.92					$12,086.04				$12,776.82
3	$10,000.00			$10,684.03					$12,573.23			$12,991.57
4	$10,000.00				$11,070.47					$12,864.89		$13,074.59
5	$10,000.00					$11,547.79						$12,718.47
	$50,000.00											**$64,066.66**
									Five-Year strategy better by:			**$2,556.07**

Getting the Best GIC rates

Finding the best GIC interest rate is worth the effort, especially when we're talking about a longer period of time. For example, a 1% increase in the average annual rate of return of a $50,000 five-year GIC to 3% from 2% over a ten-year period would build your savings to $67,196 - $6,246 higher than the $60,950 you'd end up with at 2% as follows:

Example 1

$50,000 GIC, five-year term, 2% annual rate of return, compounded annually:

Value after five years = $55,204

Value after ten years = $60,950

Example 2

$50,000 GIC, five-year term, 3% annual rate of return, compounded annually:

Value after five years = $57,964

Value after ten years = $67,196

That's over $6,000 more just for finding an interest rate that is 1% better.

So where do you go to find the best rates? Chances are your investment advisor will not want to buy GICs for you whether it's in an RRSP, TFSA or regular investment account. The reason is simple – he or she will make much more off you if you are in mutual funds.

So it will be up to you to find another way. One option is to deal directly with the banks and open up your own account with them.

To decide where the best rates are simply google "Financial Post GIC rates." There you will get a nice, summary of dozens of institutions including banks, trust companies, credit unions and life insurance companies.

I just did that on July 25, 2014 and found the following rates offered by the big six banks for non-redeemable GICs with interest paid annually (see Table 2.5):

TABLE 2.5 Rates Offered by the Big Six Banks for Non-Redeemable GICs with Interest Paid Annually

	Minimum Investment	Five-Year GIC
Bank of Montreal	$1,000	1.95%
CIBC	$1,000	1.75%
National Bank	$1,000	1.75%
Royal Bank	$1,000	2.00%
Scotiabank	$1,000	1.75%
TD Canada Trust	$1,000	2.00%

When I called one of the banks above to get further details about the non-redeemable five-year GIC rate to see if there was any flexibility in the rate the answer was "no." The website, however, did say that I could get an "online purchase/renewal bonus" of 0.50%. She said this was not available if I purchased the GIC through her on the phone.

The person then began talking about the benefits of a market-linked GIC that provided returns linked to certain market index increases over the time period. All the market-linked GICs had a maximum return amount listed but the minimum return was zero if the associated market had a negative return.

The moral of the story is that it is complicated to try to do this all yourself. Your best strategy is to educate yourself in all the GIC options before you start calling to get the best product and rate. You may also wish to consider getting some help from a deposit broker.

Consider a Deposit Broker

A deposit broker is an independent financial professional who specializes in guaranteed investment products such as GICs and term deposits.

I honestly knew very little about them until I started researching this book. I actually even had an accounting client that utilized a deposit broker to handle their GIC investments. I always wondered why it was necessary to have a broker handle something as simple as

GICs. Now I am convinced they can play an important role in your retirement plans.

Finds the Best Rates

The first important role deposit brokers fulfill is to monitor the available interest rates of various products on a daily basis to find the best possible returns. Because different products are constantly being created and because demand and activity vary daily with each financial institution, new opportunities for better rates are constantly being created.

According to one deposit broker I talked to, they can often find rates that are up to one percent better than the posted rates of the financial institutions. As we have seen, that can make a huge difference in your retirement nest-egg over the long term.

Saves Time

A deposit broker saves you the time and effort of finding the current rates of dozens of different financial institutions. While many investment advisors often prefer to sell mutual funds including money market funds issued by their own company, a deposit broker has access to many unrelated financial institutions' rates.

Advice

Even though investing in simple, no-risk GICs is not as complex as mutual funds, it is still important to get independent advice on their use. For example, for estate planning purposes you might decide the right registration is jointly with your spouse instead of in your name only. You may also need advice on what terms to renew at as you approach the age where you will need access to your money. You may also wish to have another person double check to make sure you are onside with respect to CDIC insurance limits.

You Don't Pay Fees

When purchasing GICs and other guaranteed investments through a deposit broker, you don't pay fees or commissions to your broker. There are also no "hidden fees" being taken out of your investment returns as is the case with mutual funds through the management expenses. Deposit brokers do get paid however - they receive a finder's fee directly from the institutions that you purchase the GICs from.

Who Regulates Deposit Brokers?

In Canada, the Self-Regulatory Organization (SRO) for deposit brokers is the Registered Deposit Brokers Association (RDBA) formerly known as the Federation of Canadian Independent Deposit Brokers (FCIDB). The RDBA regulates the operations and business conduct of its members and their representatives in order to protect investors and the public interest.

Incorporated in 1987 and given the mandate to represent the industry in late 2008, the RDBA is responsible for representing and organizing the industry's views, developing policies and procedures for dealing with the regulatory requirements, and for auditing member firm compliance with the rules.

According to a RDBA media release dated December 1, 2008:

Nationally, across Canada, an estimated 3,500 individuals act as or on behalf of a Deposit Broker, helping investors find the best rates for Guaranteed Investment Certificates (GICs) and other guaranteed deposit products issued by banks, trust companies and other financial institutions. Approximately $30 billion in such deposits are placed each year through this independent broker network with oversight left to each Financial Institution's independent effort. The necessity of more than 30 FI's, each complying with stringent Know Your Client (KYC) and product disclosure best practices and the various legislative acts such as AML&ATF (Money laundering), PIPEDA (Privacy) and product disclosure, places a heavy burden in administration and costs on all industry stakeholders.[1]

Remember that not all of the financial institutions represented by the broker are members of CDIC. Insurance companies are covered by Assuris (a not-for-profit organization that protects Canadian policyholders in the event that their life insurance company should fail) and credit unions are covered by provincial deposit insurance organizations.

Also beware that not all deposit brokers are registered members of the RDBA and therefore bound by its policies and procedures and code of ethics.

---

[1] www.rdba.ca

Fiscal Agents

Fiscal Agents Financial Services Group (www.fiscalagents.com) is a deposit broker registered with the RDBA. In fact Fiscal Agents' founder David Newman, was instrumental in convincing the federal government to increase the CDIC insurance coverage of bank and trust company deposits from $60,000 to $100,000.

You may have seen Fiscal Agents' charts of maximum GIC rates in the *National Post*, the *Toronto Star* or several finance-related websites.

Table 2.6 shows a summary chart that the company prepares for clients based on a review of many financial institutions' published rates, generated on July 25, 2014.

You can see that the lowest rate is 1.0% offered by Bank West, and the highest rate is 2.9% offered by Oaken Financial, a trademark of Home Trust, a CDIC member.

As we have seen, the big six banks ranged from 1.75% to 2.0%.

You will note that some of the financial institutions on the list are not covered by CDIC. Credit union deposits, for example, are guaranteed by provincially run deposit guarantee organizations. It is important to note that some credit union deposit guarantee corporations are backed by their provincial governments while others are not. This is important, as a guarantee is only as strong as the entity making the guarantee.

Outlook Financial, for example, is covered by the Credit Union Deposit Guarantee Corporation of Manitoba (http://www.cudgc.com), which is not explicitly backed by the Manitoba government. Credit unions in Ontario are covered by an organization called the Deposit Insurance Corporation of Ontario (www.dico.com), which has the backing of the provincial government. Alberta credit unions are covered by the Alberta Credit Union Deposit Guarantee Corporation (http://www.cudgc.ab.ca/), which is backed by Alberta government.

B.C. credit unions are covered by the Credit Union Deposit Insurance Corporation of B.C. (http://www.cudicbc.ca/), which is not explicitly backed by B.C. government. In Nova Scotia, the Nova Scotia Credit Union Deposit Insurance Corporation (http://www.nscudic.org/) covers credit unions there but it is not explicitly backed by the Nova Scotia government.

TABLE 2.6   Fiscal Agents GIC Rates as of July 25th, 2014

Institution	Minimum Investment in a Five-year GIC	Interest Rate on a Five-year GIC	Insured by CDIC?
Chartered Banks			
ATB Financial	$1,000	2.20%	No
Alterna Svgs/Alterna Bk	$500	2.30%	Yes
Bank of Montreal	$1,000	1.95%	Yes
Bank of Nova Scotia	$1,000	1.75%	Yes
Bank West	$5,000	1.00%	Yes
Canadian Tire Bank	$500	2.20%	Yes
Canadian Western Bank	$1,000	2.45%	Yes
CFF Bank	$5,000	2.35%	Yes
CIBC	$1,000	1.75%	Yes
Equitable Bank	$5,000	2.45%	Yes
ICICI Bank Canada	$1,000	2.85%	Yes
Manulife Bank	$2,500	2.45%	Yes
National Bank	$1,000	1.75%	Yes
President's Choice Financial	$100	2.50%	Yes
Royal Bank	$1,000	2.00%	Yes
State Bank of India (Canada)	$1,000	2.50%	Yes
TD Canada Trust	$1,000	2.00%	Yes
Tangerine	$0	2.55%	Yes
Trust and Loan Companies			
Canadian Western Trust	$5,000	2.10%	Yes
Community Trust	$5,000	2.30%	Yes
Concentra Financial	$10,000	2.00%	Yes
Effort Trust	$5,000	2.60%	Yes
Home Trust	$5,000	2.60%	Yes
Investors Group Trust	$1,000	2.05%	Yes
MCAN Mortgage Corp.	$5,000	2.30%	Yes
MTCC	$1,000	1.75%	Yes
Oaken Financial	$1,000	2.90%	Yes
Peoples Trust	$5,000	2.30%	Yes

(continued overleaf)

TABLE 2.6 *(continued)*

Institution	Minimum Investment in a Five-year GIC	Interest Rate on a Five-year GIC	Insured by CDIC?
Other Financial Institutions			
Achieva Financial	$1,000	2.60%	No
Airline Financial Credit Union	$1,000	2.60%	No
AcceleRate Financial	$1,000	2.75%	No
Canada Life	$1,000	1.70%	No
Canadian Direct Financial	$1,000	2.70%	Yes
Comtech Credit Union	$1,000	2.40%	No
Desjardins Financial Security	$500	1.95%	No
DUCA Credit Union	$500	2.60%	No
First Calgary Financial	$500	2.35%	No
First Ontario Credit Union	$1,000	2.70%	No
IC Savings	$1,000	2.45%	No
London Life	$1,000	1.70%	No
Luminus Financial	$500	2.15%	No
Manulife Investments	$2,500	2.05%	No
Meridian Credit Union	$500	2.30%	No
OUTLOOK Financial	$1,000	2.80%	No
PACE Savings & Credit Union	$1,000	2.10%	No
Parama Credit Union	$1,000	2.45%	No
Standard Life	$1,000	1.95%	No
Steinbach Credit Union	$500	2.60%	No
Sun Life Financial	$1,000	2.50%	Yes

Source: Fiscal Agents Financial Services Group, www.fiscalagents.com

Saskatchewan credit unions are covered by the Saskatchewan Credit Union Deposit Guarantee Corporation (http://www.cudgc.sk.ca), which is also not explicitly backed by Saskatchewan government

I have nothing against credit unions, they provide a legitimate alternative to the standard banks, but assuming you'd like the security of knowing your savings are guaranteed by the Federal government through the CDIC, look over the list for the maximum rate for a CDIC member when you are in the market for your next GIC.

And make sure you don't just accept your bank's posted rate. In this case why accept a rate of 1.75% to 2.0% when you can go to the competition and get 2.9% from another CDIC member? Ask them to match the rate or take your business elsewhere.

ALL ABOUT GICS

A Guaranteed Investment Certificate (GIC) is an investment security sold by Canadian banks and trust companies that provides a rate of return as well as a return of the principal amount at the end of its term. The main types are as follows.

Cashable/Non-Cashable

This is also known as redeemable/non-redeemable. If the GIC is cashable or redeemable you can cash in part or all of it before its maturity date, although there will usually be a penalty for doing this. Non-cashable or non-redeemable means you cannot cash it early even if you need the funds. Thus it is important to make sure you won't need the funds if you opt for the non-cashable type.

Interest Payment Frequency

Refers to how often interest is actually paid on a GIC. Options include monthly, annually or at the end of the term.

Compounding

Refers to how often the interest earned is added to the principal for the calculation of the next amount of interest. For example, interest could be calculated annually and paid at maturity. That means, a $1,000 GIC at 5% a year, would build to a maturity value of $1,276.28 after five years. It would be worth $1,050 at the end of year one ($1,000 × 1.05%), then $1,102.50 after year two ($1,050 × 1.05%), $1,157.63 after year three ($1,102.50 × 1.05%), $1,215.51 after year four ($1,157.63 × 1.05%) and $1,276.28 after year five ($1,215.51 × 1.05%).

Market-Linked GICs

These GICs provide returns based on the performance of a certain stock market index. The return you actually earn is usually less than 100% of the return of the index (they have to make fees somehow!) and there may not be a minimum guaranteed return. In other words, if the index actually declines during the period you'd get your principal back but no interest.

Variable Rate

These GICs have changing rates over the term of the GIC. They often start at a low rate and escalate so the final year's return looks really good but the average return is usually similar to what you could get with a fixed interest rate.

Minimum Investment Amount

This is the lowest amount you'll need to invest to open up an account.

GIC Rates of the Future

There is uncertainly about the future returns the stock market will yield but there is also uncertainty about where interest rates will go. There is an important difference though: interest rates cannot go below zero and the stock market most definitely can.

That's why the strategies in this book will focus on fixed income products, namely GICs. We are in a period of the lowest interest rates in history. The governments have to keep interest rates low to stimulate the economy. How long will they stay this low? No one knows, but the likelihood is at least for the few years it probably will take for the economy to recover fully.

Throughout this book, I will focus on rates that are available now on the assumption that interest rates will remain low for an extended period of time. This goes with my conservative philosophy. I don't want you to base your retirement plans purely on hope. I'd like you to plan based on logic, and maybe get pleasantly surprised if future returns end up being higher.

For example, do you know what annual interest rate a five-year GIC was paying in 1980? It was 12.36%. The average five-year GIC annual interest rate over the period 1980 to 2000 was 9.04%. Maybe those rates will appear again, but it's best not to base a retirement strategy on that possibility.

BUY A HOME AND PAY OFF THE MORTGAGE

Which is more valuable, an RRSP (or RRIF) worth $400,000, or a house worth $400,000?

From a simple tax point of view, you'd be better off with the house, and I'll tell you why.

The reason is that the funds in the RRSP/RRIF are pre-tax. You can't spend an RRSP or RRIF. You have to withdraw the funds and report the amount on your income tax return and pay tax on it. If you withdrew all $400,000 at once, a lot of it would be in the highest tax bracket. You'd only get to keep the amount left after tax. In Ontario in 2014 that would be approximately only $235,000.

This is because you got a tax refund in the first place when you made the RRSP contributions over the years.

We're going to look at the advantages of owning a house over an RRSP but let me be clear: not everyone can afford a house, and even if you can, you'll probably also need an RRSP to fund your retirement.

Gains in Value are Tax-Free

The increase in value of your principal residence is not taxed as it occurs, and the difference between what you paid for your home and what you sell it for – the capital gain – is not taxed when you sell. The increase in value of an RRSP/RRIF is also not taxed as it grows, but it is taxed when you withdraw it and it's taxed as regular income.

This is an important point to think about. If you own stocks or equity mutual funds in an RRSP, the capital gain on their sale is not taxed at 50% of the gain as in a normal investment account. The whole amount is taxed as regular income upon withdrawal. This is why the rule of thumb is to hold equities outside in a regular investment account.

We'll delve more into this in chapter 10 on the alternatives to RRSPs.

Source of Cash

One of the drawbacks of owning a home is that a house is not a good source of ready cash. In other words, it's not a "liquid" investment. You can't sell a little piece of it if you need some money. In fact owning a home will cost you cash to finance and maintain it.

But it can be used as collateral on a loan. This usually results in a lower interest rate because the financial institution loaning you the money has some security – if you default, they can force a sale of your home to recover the money you owe them.

But be careful here. A lot of Canadians are adopting the strategy of borrowing against their home using a Home Equity Line of Credit (HELOC) and are getting in way over their heads. Too much debt, even when it's "good debt" related to an appreciating asset, can be fatal to your financial health.

Source of Retirement Funds

I have heard more than a few stories about retired people needing to live in a retirement or nursing home when they become unable to look after themselves. Selling the principal residence at that time can be an excellent source of tax-free funds. In many cases it's the only way they could pay for it, as there are simply not enough savings.

I often get asked about reverse mortgages for retired people who are cash-poor but house-rich. It sounds like a good idea. You get to keep the house, borrow the money against it, and the loan only has to get paid back when you sell the house or pass away.

To be honest, I have never known anyone that has used one. But the research I have done has indicated several problems. First of all, the interest rates are usually quite high. There are also fees involved and I have read newspaper articles about people losing their homes in certain circumstances even though it was promised that this couldn't happen. Also, the contracts are exceedingly complicated and long. It's a case of "buyer-beware."

It would seem much simpler, cheaper and less risky to take out a secured loan using your home as collateral. But do this before you need the money, ideally before you retire. The banks are great at handing out umbrellas when it's sunny, but not after the rain starts!

Should I Buy a House?

If you don't already own a house you have a big decision to make. We'll discuss whether you can afford one next, but think about whether owning a home is right for you. If you like to move a lot, you may not wish to tie yourself down to one location.

If you are required to move, you'll have to consider the risk of rising and falling home prices. For example, if the company you work for has a habit of relocating you, it may not be worth the risk of getting burned with a badly timed sale. Some companies have stopped guaranteeing employees that they won't lose on selling a house because of relocation. It's just too costly for them. In that case, you may decide not to accept the risk of losing out personally – remember point number one of The Antidote: avoid the potential for personal financial disasters.

You may also enjoy renting because you don't have to worry about repairs and maintenance. I have lived in three different homes over a twenty-five year period and I can tell you there is always something that needs replacement or repair. It may be the furnace or air conditioner, new roof shingles, basement waterproofing or expensive plumbing or electrical work. Not to mention the standard chores like cutting the grass, shoveling the driveway and doing the gardening.

CAN I AFFORD A HOUSE?

After you decide you'd like the security and peace of mind that comes with owning a house, you'll need to determine whether or not you can afford one.

When you apply for a mortgage, lenders usually rely on two rules to determine how much you can afford to pay. They are the Gross Debt Service and Total Debt Service ratios.

Gross Debt Service Ratio (GDS)

This rule says that your monthly housing costs should not exceed 32% of your gross household monthly income. Your gross household monthly income is the salary (before deductions for income taxes, Canada Pension plan [CPP] and Employment Insurance [EI]) of you and your spouse. If you are self-employed it is your gross sales less business expenses before deductions. You also include any other sources of income, like investments and other non-employment income.

Your monthly housing costs include the mortgage payments (principal plus interest), property taxes and heating expenses.

Total Debt Service Ratio (TDS)

This rule states that your total monthly debt load should not be more than 40% of your gross monthly income. Your monthly debt load includes mortgage payments and other debt payments like car loans, credit cards, lines of credit and student loans.

JUST HOW MUCH HOUSE CAN YOU AFFORD?

The maximum price you can afford depends on several factors, including your household income, the down payment amount and the interest rate on the mortgage.

The Canadian Mortgage and Housing Corporation (CMHC) provides a lot of very useful information for potential home buyers. To give you an idea of the maximum price you can afford based on the GDS and TDS ratios, they provide an online calculator called the Mortgage Affordability Calculator at http://www.cmhc-schl.gc.ca/en/co/buho/ buho_020.cfm. This is a great tool to use as you start considering the biggest purchase of your life.

I just used it with the following information:

Gross monthly household income	$5,000
Monthly property taxes	$300
Monthly heating costs	$80
Mortgage interest rate	4%
Monthly debt payments (other than mortgage)	$500
Monthly condominium fees	$0
Down payment	$15,000
Amortization period	25 years

Here is what the calculator came up with:

Maximum mortgage	$212,920
Maximum house price	$227,920
Maximum monthly mortgage payment	$1,120.00
CMHC mortgage loan insurance premium	$6,706.97

Saving For the Down Payment

This is the hardest part of realizing your dream of home ownership. The amount you need to save could be daunting. Looking at a $300,000 house? Even a 5% down payment is $15,000. This is not going to be easy, but if you don't do it you'll never own a home.

Of course there may be other sources, including a gift from a parent, but when you think about it, the process of trying to save for a down payment is a valuable lesson in itself. That's because home ownership is going to be more expensive than renting. That extra amount of money you are trying to save as you continue to rent will probably be needed after you buy the house. In other words, you'll be forced to live on less income, which will be the case after you buy a home.

Buying With Less Than 20% Down

Currently in Canada you can buy a home with less than a 20% down payment; in fact, as little as 5% is allowed. There is a catch, however: you'll have to buy mortgage loan insurance, also known as mortgage default insurance.

Mortgage loan insurance protects the lender – your bank – in case you default and can't pay your mortgage. You may pay for the insurance in a lump sum, or you usually can have it added to the mortgage and pay it over the term of the mortgage.

Be careful not to confuse it with life insurance. With simple life insurance, the beneficiary of the deceased can choose to pay off the balance of the mortgage if the person who took out the mortgage were to die.

WARNING: Mortgage Companies Love Selling Mortgage Life Insurance!

Be careful of this trap. Some mortgage companies will try to talk you into buying their mortgage life insurance. It often looks like a small amount and they can easily add it to your mortgage payment. Check the fine print, though. In most cases they don't reduce the premium even though your mortgage principal balance is declining. In other words, if you sign up for a $300,000 mortgage, and over the years pay it down to, say, $150,000, you'd think the premiums would decline by about 50% because the mortgage life insurance would only cover the mortgage balance – $150,000 not $300,000 in this case. But that's usually not the case as the premiums remain the same as at the beginning.

A better option is just to make sure your regular life insurance policy has a sufficient death benefit to pay off the balance of your mortgage and provide for your dependents. By the way, make it a term insurance policy, not whole or universal life, as it's much cheaper and simpler.

Mortgage loan insurance in Canada is currently provided by three organizations:

- **Canada Mortgage and Housing Corporation**. CMHC is Canada's national housing agency, established as a

government-owned corporation in 1946 to address Canada's post-war housing shortage. http://www.cmhc-schl.gc.ca.
- **Genworth Canada.** The largest private residential mortgage insurer in Canada that has been around for almost two decades. http://www.genworth.ca
- **Canada Guarantee.** Entered the market in 2010 as the only 100% Canadian-owned private mortgage insurer. http://www.canadaguaranty.ca

Most mortgage loan companies require borrowers to finance the down payment from their own resources, such as gifts from relatives, RRSPs or savings. For down payments between 5% and 20%, CMHC allows lenders to offer borrowers the option of using other sources, such as loans and lender incentives. The qualifying criteria and availability of these options vary depending on the lender.

If you have less than a 20% down payment, the CMHC premiums you'll currently have to pay are shown in Table 3.1:

TABLE 3.1   CMHC Premiums Based on a Down Payment of Less than 20%

CMHC Premiums	
Loan-to-value	**Premium on Total Loan**
Up to and including 80%	1.25%
Up to and including 85%	1.80%
Up to and including 90%	2.40%
Up to and including 95%	3.15%
90.01% to 95% – non-traditional down payment	3.35%

Note that the financing required as a percentage of the total cost of the property is called the loan-to-value ratio or LTV.

So for example if you wanted to buy a home for $300,000 and had a 10% down payment ($30,000) and therefore needed to finance 90% ($270,000) the premium would be $6,480 (2.4% of $270,000).

If you were able to come up with a down payment of 15% ($45,000) and therefore needed to finance only 85% ($255,000), the premium would only be $4,590 (1.8% of $255,000).

Note that mortgage loan insurance is now only available on properties purchased for less than $1,000,000 and that mortgage loan insurance premiums in Manitoba, Ontario and Quebec are subject to provincial sales tax, which cannot be added to the loan amount.

Pre-Approved Mortgages

It's a great idea to get pre-approved for a mortgage. This simply means that before you buy a house, you find a lending institution and get them to investigate your financial situation in order to give you a guaranteed mortgage up to a certain amount.

There is nothing more stressful financially than finding the house of your dreams and sitting on pins and needles wondering if your bank will approve your mortgage and allow you to move in. Trust me, I've been there.

Going through this step can also save an incredible amount of wasted time if your search takes you into a price range that you cannot afford.

If you are pre-approved, the lender will give you a written certificate indicating the amount, the interest rate and the length of time it is good for.

Remember to bring the following to the potential lender:

- personal identity confirmation like driver's licence
- details regarding your salary or self-employment earnings (latest T4 from employment, Notices of Assessment from Canada Revenue Agency)
- a listing of your net worth – your assets (bank accounts, RRSPs, cars, etc.) and your debts (lines of credit, credit cards, bank loans)
- amount of down payment you have and where it is coming from
- details as to how you'll pay the closing costs, including legal fees and land transfer tax (these fees are often between 1.5% and 4% of the purchase price)

What if I don't qualify?

Your calculations may indicate that you'll have problems getting approved for a mortgage based on your income and financial situation. The CMHC has the following suggestions:

- work first on paying down your existing debt
- wait to save a larger down payment
- look for a less expensive house
- meet with a credit counsellor who can help get your spending and debt under control
- buy your home through a rent-to-own program provided by the builder, a non-profit sponsor or a government sponsor
- find out about programs through which you can help build your own home
- ask the housing department of your municipality about any special programs available

One of the first things a potential lender will do to decide whether to loan you any money is to check your credit report. It's therefore vital that you know all about it.

YOUR CREDIT REPORT

Your credit report is a history of your credit activities that lenders obtain from a credit reporting agency commonly known as a credit bureau. Credit bureaus rely on information gathered from credit grantors (banks, credit card companies, retail stores, etc.) and public records (legal judgments, etc.) to make their determinations.

When you sign for a consumer loan, credit card, lease for a car, or line of credit, you are permitting the credit grantors to share the credit information with the appropriate credit reporting bureaus.

You have the right to see what's on your credit report and you should do this before you give a lender the right to ask for it so you can improve it if necessary and make any corrections that are required.

There are two credit bureaus or credit reporting agencies in Canada. They both allow you to obtain a copy of your credit report and credit score as well as an analysis of your personal credit situation. You must provide personal information during the order process for your credit information so that your identity can be verified. They are:

- **Equifax Canada Inc.** http://ww.equifax.ca
- **TransUnion of Canada.** http://www.transunion.ca

What is in a Credit Report

A credit report contains the basic identification information, including your name, address, date of birth, current employment information, as well as your Social Insurance Number. It usually doesn't include your credit score, which you'll need to pay extra to obtain. We'll discuss one of the most common credit scores, the Fico score, in a few minutes.

Here's what your credit report includes:

- credit information reported by creditors to the reporting agency on existing debts
- overall comments on your historical credit performance
- any bankruptcy
- voluntary deposit – orderly payment of debt, credit counselling
- any registered consumer proposals
- judgments, seizure of movables/immovables, garnishment of wages
- secured loans (court name, date filed and creditor's name)
- collection accounts
- list of inquiries from creditors relating to credit applications you have made
- public court reports

Information reported by credit grantors often include:

- phone number of the credit grantor
- account number
- type of account (revolving like a credit card or installment like a car lease)
- date opened
- months reviewed (how long you have had it)
- status (paid as agreed or not)

- payment history (if any minimum required payments have been late)
- credit limit
- payment amount (minimum payment for credit cards, monthly lease amounts of car leases)
- balance amount (how much was owing the last time the credit grantor reported)
- past due amount (if any)
- date of last activity
- date reported
- other comments (e.g. monthly payments)

How to Get a Free Copy of Your Credit Report

You can get a copy of your credit report mailed to you free of charge from either of the credit bureaus. All it takes is a five-minute phone call.

Just call Equifax at 1–800–465–7166. The automated telephone system will ask you to enter your Social Insurance Number (SIN), street number, apartment number (if applicable), postal code and a major credit card number if you have one.

TransUnion also allows you to order your credit report (they call it a "consumer disclosure") by phone using their interactive voice response system. The number is 1–800–663–9980. They will ask you the same questions as Equifax.

Both organizations say the report will then be mailed to your home address in about five days. I just ordered mine from both and they came as promised.

Getting Your Credit Report Online

If you'd like your credit report right away you can order it online from Equifax. For $23.95 you can get:

- your credit score
- your personalized credit report
- a full explanation of your score and how lenders view your credit risk

- tips on how you can improve your credit score
- custom graphs showing how you rank versus other Canadians
- specific factors that most affect your credit score

For $15.50 you can receive your credit report with tips about how to improve it, but you won't receive your credit score.

At TransUnion, it seems you have to sign up for credit monitoring for $16.95 a month to get unlimited updates to your credit report and score, email updates of critical changes to your credit report as well as personalized debt analysis.

What is a FICO Credit Score?

The FICO score was developed by Fair, Isaac and Company, often referred to as the pioneer of credit scoring. It's a number between 300 and 900 that lenders use to judge your credit risk. It is important to note that it's a snapshot of your credit risk at a point in time. Your score changes depending on your financial activities over time. The higher your credit score, the more likely you are to be approved for loans and to receive favourable interest rates when you are approved.

What Affects Your Credit Score?

Your credit score is affected by many things but most important are the following:

- number of accounts not paid as agreed
- total credit balance related to total credit limits available
- whether credit lines revolve regularly or whether they remain fully utilized
- number of credit inquiries made in the last year by creditors
- existence of judgments, executions and writs in the public records

An Important Warning:

There is one other important thing about your credit rating. Your score could be low even if you are well off and earn a good salary. If you are not aware of this it could lead to major problems. Let me give you an example.

I knew a woman who made over $170,000 a year and had no credit card balance, nor any other consumer debt. She also owned a house worth about $1,000,000 with a mortgage of less than half that. But you know what? Her credit rating was so low she could not even get a credit card. That's because the credit card she used was in her husband's name. It was a secondary card of his and her use of it was not building her own credit rating.

The problem was that if her husband were to die, she would have been left in a very difficult financial situation – unable to get credit of any kind. In her case the answer was to shop around and find an institution willing to give her a basic card, and then begin using it. She did this and was sure to pay the minimum balance on time each and every month. In fact she made sure she paid off the balance every month. Within two years her credit rating improved dramatically and the problem was solved.

Note that if this is your situation you may have to apply for a secured credit card where you put money up front as collateral against any credit limit you are given. In this way, the financial institution can't lose because if you default on your payments, they simply keep your deposit.

How to Improve Your Credit Score

If your credit score needs improving, the most important steps you can take include:

- **Pay your bills on time.** Pay them a day or so early if you can, because if they are even a day or two late it affects your score.
- **Pay down the balance.** The higher the balance and the closer you are to your credit limits, the lower your score.
- **Limit the amount of credit you apply for.** Each creditor makes an inquiry and excess inquiries reduce your rating.
- **Pay down lines of credit periodically.** Even if you have to draw them back up later, pay them down when you can to show positive activity.

- **Be careful with your credit cards.** Lost credit cards are a major source of credit problems. Check that you have them all from time to time and if you ever lose one, report it immediately to the credit card company. If you don't you could be on the hook for a lot of money that you did not spend.

YOUR HOME AS AN INVESTMENT

Remember we decided that we'd rather have a home worth $400,000 than an RRSP/RRIF worth the same amount? Well, there are other reasons besides the tax one. They include those ugly DSC fees to cash out your RRSP/RRIF if the investments were in mutual funds. What if your RRSP was worth $400,000 in June of 2008 and was invested substantially in equities? After fees over the past six years it's probably not even worth that amount today.

It's true that a house can also decline in value and investing in a house because it appreciates in value is never a 100% guarantee, but for many people it's the best investment they will ever make.

Let's move on to another real-life story about the housing strategy.

"The Best Investment I Ever Made"

In researching this chapter I asked a couple of individuals in the "seasoned" category – roughly eighty years old – what their best financial move was. Both immediately replied "my houses."

I found that a little surprising for several reasons. First of all, both individuals had spent their working years (the fifties to the nineties) in the prime bull years of the stock market – the post-World War II era – and invested predominately in equities. One, whom I'll call Joe, even worked the majority of his career in the investment industry. Here's an investment professional who had daily access to financial information because it was his job, able to invest with little or no fees to drag him down, during the heyday of stocks, and his best move was his house-buying strategy. Interesting eh?

HERE'S JOE'S STORY:

In 1951 when I graduated from the University of Western Ontario, a friend's parent died and their house sold for $8,000. I remember thinking at the time that was not much changed from the value in the 1930s, but perhaps it was $3,000 then!

Jill and I moved to New York in 1962 and rented a one-bedroom flat in the centre of Manhattan on East 81st Street for $300 per month, which I remember was roughly twice the going rate for larger, two-bedroom flats in Toronto! I pleaded with my business partners in Toronto to subsidize me, to no avail. I was earning at the rate of $16,000 per annum. Not bad, as I later found out.

We moved to London, England in 1968 and came back to Toronto in 1974 – renting all that time. A centre-hall-plan house that I looked at on Douglas Drive in Rosedale in 1972 that was $50,000 had risen in value to over $100,000 in 1974. We had gone through rampant inflation at a rate of 12% plus in 1971 and it was still with us. By 1974 it didn't look like things were going to get cheaper so we bought a house for $174,000 (a one-hundred-year-old on South Drive), largely financed with a bank loan borrowed against my investment company shares (good as gold!). In 1972 we had received a 100% dividend, which made an enormous difference. It was not to happen again!

Inflation of house prices continued and we wanted to move, so we sold the house in 1978/9 for $309,000 and bought one (a converted bungalow in North Rosedale) for $264,000. I can thank my wife for that.

This is hard to believe, but we sold that house in 1987 for $779,000.

Many well-off people moved into this desirable area, partly because a senior Ontario politician bought a house around the corner from me on Douglas (one that looked very much like the one I looked at in 1972 for $50,000) for $1,000,000 or very close to it. The house of my family lawyer's mother, a modest two-story on Douglas was sold for $1,000,000 (right across the street from the politician's house) and one 300 feet from it was sold to another individual for $1,000,000. I said at the time, "I don't think we can afford to live here anymore," particularly as I had left the investment company and I was seriously thinking about, and subsequently did, resign from the other investment firm I had joined, because I thought that the U.S. owners were going to sewer the U.S. firm as well as the Canadian one. They did.

(continued)

(continued)

So in 1987 we sold the Toronto house, and bought this house in Oakville for $439,000 and put the balance in the investment account. Not that it matters, but the house is supposed to be in the $800,000 to $900,000 range now.

All boats rise in an up market, and historically, we have been in one for fifty-odd years … rising at different rates over the years but nonetheless rising. Pressure of population increase drives it, certainly in the real estate market, but it always gets ahead of itself and corrects, sometimes for a very long time. The approximately 20% decline from 1987 to 1995 approximately is a good example. We are in one of those periods now, I believe.

Let's summarize the gains Joe has realized since 1974. In 1978 his gain was $135,000, in 1987 he had a gain of $515,000 and in 2008 his unrealized gain was $361,000, assuming the low end of his value estimate. The total gain over the years? More than $1 million – $1,011,000, actually. And it was all tax free. See Figure 3.1

FIGURE 3.1   Joe's Gains from 1974 to 2008

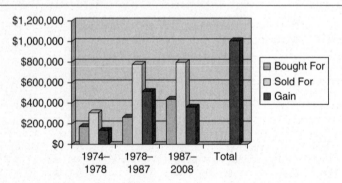

Obviously we have no idea if this trend will continue for the housing market, but when I compare it to the volatility of the stock market, personally I'd put my money in bricks and mortar.

CONCLUSION

Assuming you can afford it, an investment in your house is tough to beat. Sure your house may rise and fall in value but these fluctuations usually aren't as gut wrenching as the peaks and valleys of the stock market. Over the long term, it's often the best investment most people make.

REDUCING EXPENSES DOESN'T HAVE TO BE PAINFUL

Almost everyone tells us to watch the small expenses. Save the pennies and the dollars will look after themselves. Skip a coffee a day and you'll get rich. It's all a load of bunk. A few pennies or even dollars saved here and there won't add up to a hill of beans. And what's worse, those little things are often what makes life great: an intimate meal at a cozy restaurant, a steaming Tim Hortons Double Double, a cherry float on a hot summer's day. There's got to be a better way than giving up life's simple pleasures!

Why not focus your energy on reducing what are probably two of your largest expenses while not having to sacrifice anything? You can, and it's quite easy.

Those expenses are interest and taxes.

REDUCING THE INTEREST YOU PAY

Unfortunately, as soon as we get out of high school, life starts to get expensive. We want to go to university, and that brings tuition fees, food, lodging, and other expenses. Often, people have to go into debt with student loans simply to afford the education.

Next may come some traveling – say, to Europe. OK, but that's going to cost you. Add to the student debt.

Want to get married? Add the expenses for things like the ring, the reception and the honeymoon. . . .

Want to live somewhere other than your parents' house? You'll probably need a mortgage to pay for your dream home.

Maybe some kids would be good to have around. Do yourself a favour: Don't do a cash flow projection to determine if they are a good idea. They cause big cash outflows!

The result? In our late twenties or early thirties (usually) we end up with a mortgage, possibly a line of credit, a car loan, and maybe some credit card debt. And that's assuming we've paid off the student loan – and as yet another fallout from the Great Recession, this is less likely now than it used to be.

All that debt means we pay a lot of interest each and every year. It simply makes sense to focus on minimizing our interest expenses, because they are often among our biggest cash drains. I call the years between moving out on our own until the debts are all paid off *the spending years*.

The Spending Years

Reducing interest expenses during the spending years is the key to getting ahead. There are two ways to reduce the interest you pay:

1. Reduce the amount of the debt.
2. Reduce the interest rate on the debt.

To reduce the interest rate, for example, if you are in credit card debt paying punishing interest of 20 percent or more a year, simply changing to a basic no frills card at prime plus a percent or two could save you thousands of dollars a year.

But let's start with the more significant one – reducing the amount of the debt itself.

Reducing the Amount of the Debt

Obviously, the more debt we have, the greater the amount of interest we'll have to pay on that debt. Reducing the principal amount of the debt should be your number one goal.

During the spending years, this is going to be difficult. There are many demands for money and deciding to cut back on one area or another will probably be hard, but it is the most important step to gaining control of your finances and setting yourself up for a comfortable retirement.

The first step to achieving this goal of reducing debt is to know what your debt balance is. Do you even know? Do yourself a favour and figure it out right now.

Go and get last month's statements for your mortgage, car loan, line of credit and any credit cards, as well as any other debts you might have and start a table. List all these debts in the first column. Then, list the principal balance of each in the second column, the total payment you made last month in the third, the interest portion of that payment in the fourth, the interest you'll pay in the next year in the fifth, the years left on the loan in the sixth, and the interest rate in the seventh.

The interest you'll pay in the next year will probably be the hardest to calculate unless you have a payment schedule from your bank or finance company for any fixed-term loans like mortgages and car loans. This "amortization schedule" should show the principal balance and the principal and interest portion of each payment. For variable rate loans with open terms, simply multiply the average balance of the loan times the interest rate. For many people this will be a real eye-opener because they simply haven't ever done this before – they don't know how much debt they are in.

Let's try doing it for someone we'll call Jimmy. His chart is shown in Table 4.1.

The first thing to notice about Jimmy is that he's been spending more than he makes because he has consumer debt he can't pay off. He has $10,000 on an unsecured line of credit charging 7.5 percent a year and $11,000 on a credit card at 20% interest. If Jimmy continues to spend more than he makes, his plans for a nice retirement are in jeopardy.

Just look at what it is costing him. The interest paid annually on his line of credit and credit card is $2,950 ($750 on the line of credit and $2,200 on the credit card). That's almost $3,000 down the toilet each year.

TABLE 4.1 Jimmy's Chart

Type of Debt	Principal Balance	Total Payment Last Month	Interest Paid Last Month	Interest Paid Annually	Years Left on Loan	Interest Rate
Five-year mortgage	$150,000	$1,075	$750	$8,891	20	6%
Car loan	$15,000	$366	$100	$1,080	4	8%
Line of credit	$10,000	$200	$63	$750	5	7.5%
Credit card	$11,000	$291	$183	$2,200	5	20%
Total	$186,000	$1,932	$1,096	$12,921		

How long before he'll have the line of credit and credit card paid off? Five years. So he'll end up wasting about $15,000 in interest if he continues his current habits.

But here's the real problem: His current debt will take five years to pay off *if he doesn't add anything else to it.*

The real problem most people have, Jimmy included, is that their lifestyles demand that they keep spending as they have in the past. For example, Jimmy could pay down his credit card by $1,000 one month, but if he can't resist putting that big screen TV on it for $1,500, he'll end up worse off by $500 plus the additional interest.

I know that sounds simple, and it is – it's a simple concept – but changing your lifestyle will be tough for anyone that has debt balances.

Reducing the Interest Rate on the Debt

OK, I think you get my drift. Let's get back to you and your situation. You want to reduce the interest you pay on your debt.

The most important thing you can do is make sure your credit rating is as high as possible. The better it is, the easier it will be for you to shop around for the best interest rate, because lenders will be bidding against each other for your business. That puts you in the driver's seat.

The other thing you can do to reduce the interest you pay on the debt you have is to restructure it.

Let's take Jimmy, for example. The first thing he should do is rank his debt from highest interest rate to lowest. The credit card debt comes out on top at 20 percent. He should reduce his payments on any lower-interest debt that he can and apply the excess to the credit card debt.

But interestingly, here is where the financial institutions have the advantage. He simply can't reduce his mortgage payments – the debt with the lowest interest rate. Jimmy happens to be locked in for the next five years. He has no choice but to continue to make the payments each and every month on his mortgage, while the bank lets him pay a small minimum balance on his high-interest credit card. Gee, thanks!

He can, however, reduce the payments on his line of credit at 7.5 percent to the lowest amount possible and increase the amount he pays on his credit card. He should also call his bank and at least several other credit card issuers to replace his gold card with a more basic one. Competitors will often offer a low rate on a balance transfer to attract new clients.

Debt Consolidation

WARNING: The following strategy *could* be dangerous to your financial health!

Debt consolidation is the process of taking your existing debt and combining it into one loan at a lower interest rate.

Jimmy could apply to see if he could combine his line of credit and credit card debt into one loan, possibly secured by his house, to reduce the interest rate.

US consumers, however, have provided us with a glimpse of how this strategy can be a financial killer. Many borrowed up to the limit on the value of their home, continued to spend more than they made, and ran up their credit cards and lines of credit again. Then the housing market declined and they were left with a mortgage worth more than their home, as well as other debt. This is a personal financial disaster of epic proportions.

Get Three Quotes

Well-run businesses always get at least a few quotes for large purchases of goods or services. Why should you be any different? Call at least three financial institutions when it comes time to renew your mortgage, line of credit, etc. This will ensure the competitive bid process is used to get the best rate available.

DEBT AND THE ECONOMY

When you think about it, what we have just talked about is cause for very real concern these days. If many consumers have been spending more than they make, buying goods and services they can't afford, and this keeps the economy humming, what happens when they hit their breaking point? What happens when they can't borrow any more because their debt levels are maxed out?

Isn't that what just happened in the United States in the fall of 2008? The consequences have been very ugly. Companies started to report huge losses as sales dove, with hundreds of thousands of job losses as a result. People couldn't make their payments and mortgages and loans defaulted at record pace. Many people were forced to sell their homes at fire-sale rates, or were foreclosed on, as house prices plummeted.

What's worse is that the problem was not contained within the United States. It seems people worldwide followed the same debt-acquiring strategy – they wanted the good life, too.

How are they trying to fix the problem? The United States and governments all over the world are pumping more money into the system by basically printing it, loaning it to the banks, and asking them to loan it to consumers. Well, I guess that's all they can do, but it sounds too easy to me.

Isn't the real problem that in much of US industry, costs are too high and demand for the goods is low? Shouldn't the focus be on the businesses starting to work more efficiently, producing what consumers want, rather than governments bailing them out with cash infusions and trying to force banks to loan people money to continue to spend more than they make buying things they don't need?

The governments can play economic games like printing more money and keeping interest rates at historical lows to encourage people to spend when they are already spending more than they make, and bailing out companies by investing in them, but ultimately will this do anything other than delay the inevitable? It's like putting a bandage on a severely broken leg. It might help but it doesn't solve the basic problem – the leg is still broken.

Put another way, trying to keep a bubble from bursting by pumping more air into it will result in a big bang sooner or later.

REDUCING TAXES

Nobody likes to pay taxes, and reducing them should be on everyone's mind. What could be less painful than a simple switch of two numbers on you and your spouse's tax returns that reduces the taxes you pay by a thousand dollars?

That's one reason I recommend that you pay to have a professional prepare your income tax returns. If you don't and you miss certain opportunities, it could cost you dearly. I also recommend that you pay a professional to make a detailed analysis of your family's tax situation, with an eye to reducing taxes. This is obviously more beneficial if your financial life is at all complicated. You might find it money very well spent. Let's start with the basics.

How to Calculate Your Tax Bill

Why wait until April of the next year to find out how much tax you owe or what refund you'll get for the prior year? Most people do just that – wait until the tax preparer has completed their tax return to give them the good or bad news about their refund or balance owing. That's a mistake. The sooner you start thinking about your tax bill, the more likely it is that you will be able to make adjustments to save you tax.

It's easy to do your own calculations at any time using a free tool on a Canada Revenue Agency (CRA) website. The advantage to this is that it's easy to play with the figures to see the effect of any of the strategies we'll be talking about.

Try it now. Use an online search engine to find a "payroll deductions online calculator." or go to http://www.cra-arc.gc.ca/esrvc-srvce/tx/bsnss/pdoc-eng.html.

The program operates on the website, so there's no need to download it to your computer and worry about whether it will work on your operating system. It calculates payroll deductions for all provinces (except for Quebec) and territories based on information you provide. To perform calculations for Quebec, you'll need to download the WINRAS program from Revenu Quebec (search "Winras Revenu Quebec") or go to http://www.revenuquebec.ca/en/sepf/services/sgp_winras/default.aspx.

All you have to do is enter the following information:

- Province or territory of employment
- Date the employee is paid
- The number of pay periods in the year as follows:
  - daily (240 pay periods a year)
  - weekly (52 pay periods a year)
  - biweekly (26 pay periods a year)
  - semi-monthly (24 pay periods a year)
  - monthly (12 pay periods a year)
  - 10 pay periods a year
  - 13 pay periods a year
  - 22 pay periods a year
  - weekly (53 pay periods a year)
  - biweekly (27 pay periods a year)

You can also enter the employee and employer's name, which are optional fields.

If you know your gross salary and the amount of any taxable benefits you are receiving, you should be able to duplicate your pay stub details from your employer.

This can reveal some interesting details about your tax situation.

Happy New Year – Here's Your Reduced Paycheck

Ever wonder why your net pay seems to decline at the beginning of a new calendar year, even though you may have received a raise? That's because you start over again, having to make CPP and EI payments. In other words, as soon as your gross salary exceeds the CPP and EI limits ($52,500 and $48,600, respectively, for 2014) in a calendar year you will have had the maximum CPP and EI amount already withheld for that year. All your paychecks past that point will not have any CPP or EI withheld. The withholdings for the new year start with the first paycheck dated in the new year.

Let's look at an example. Say that you earned an annual gross salary of $80,000 including any taxable benefits, in Ontario in 2014, and that you get paid monthly. In this case, in the CRA's program, select Ontario as the province, monthly pay periods and January 31, 2014, as the date the employee is paid, then click "Next."

On the next screen, enter the amount of the monthly gross salary – $6,666.67 in this case ($80,000/12) for the salary or wages income per pay period and select no bonus or retroactive payment. Then click "Next."

On the next screen, enter other items including CPP and EI amounts deducted year-to-date, as well as federal and provincial claim code amounts (the total nonrefundable tax credits you'll be claiming for the year). We'll assume it's the first paycheck of the year and therefore no CPP or EI have been withheld yet and only the basic personal exemption (Claim code 1) applies federally and provincially.

Here's what the program comes up with when we click "Calculate:

Payroll Deductions Online Calculator
Result

Employee's name:			
Employer's name:			
Pay period frequency:	Monthly (12 pay periods a year)		
Date the employee is paid:	2014-01-31 (YYYY-MM-DD)		
Province of employment:	Ontario		
Federal amount from TD1:	Minimum - 11,138.00 (Claim code 1)		
Provincial amount from TD1:	Minimum - 9,670.00 (Claim code 1)		
Salary or wages income		6,666.67	
Total cash income			**6,666.67**
Taxable income for the pay period		6,666.67	
Pensionable earnings for the pay period		6,666.67	
Insurable earnings for the pay period		6,666.67	
Federal tax deduction	1,015.20		
Provincial tax deduction	492.12		
Total tax deductions		1,507.32	
CPP deductions		315.56	
EI deductions		125.33	
Total deductions			**1,948.21**
Net amount			**4,718.46**

As you can see, your net pay would have been $4,718.46 after deductions of $315.56 for CPP and $125.33 for EI. After August, your gross salary to date will have exceeded the CPP and EI maximums, so for the months of September to December 2014 your net pay would have increased to $5,159.35 (gross of $6,666.67 less total taxes of $1,507.32).

The real benefit of this program, however, is that it also allows you to calculate your tax figures for an entire year. I find the easiest way to do this is to enter $0.01 as your gross income and enter your entire salary as a bonus.

In the example we have just looked at, if we enter $0.01 as the monthly salary and $80,000 as the bonus, here's what we get:

Payroll Deductions Online Calculator
Result

Employee's name:			
Employer's name:			
Pay period frequency:	Monthly (12 pay periods a year)		
Date the employee is paid:	2014-01-31 (YYYY-MM-DD)		
Province of employment:	Ontario		
Federal amount from TD1:	Minimum - 11,138.00 (Claim code 1)		
Provincial amount from TD1:	Minimum - 9,670.00 (Claim code 1)		
Salary or wages income		0.01	
Cash income			**0.01**
Federal tax deduction	0.00		
Provincial tax deduction	0.00		
Total tax deductions		0.00	
CPP deductions		0.00	
EI deductions		0.01	
Total deductions on income			**0.01**
Total current bonus payable			**80,000.00**
Federal tax deduction on bonus	12,182.40		
Provincial tax deduction on bonus	5,905.45		
Total tax deductions on bonus		18,087.85	
CPP deductions on bonus		2,425.50	
EI deductions on bonus		913.67	
Total deductions on bonus			**21,427.02**
Total deductions on income and bonus			**21,427.03**
Net amount			**58,572.98**

There is your answer – net pay of $58,572.98 after tax of $18,087.85, CPP of $2,425.50, and EI of 913.67.

Now the interesting part. What if you got a $10,000 bonus? Simply change the bonus from $80,000 to $90,000 and you'll find out your tax bill would go up to $21,916.02, resulting in net pay of $64,744.81 (CPP and EI deductions remain the same since they are at the maximum already). Your taxes rose by $3,828.17 and you got to keep $6,171.83 of your $10,000 bonus.

Marginal Tax Rates

We often hear the term *marginal tax rate* with respect to taxes and it's vital that you know exactly what that is. It is the extra amount of tax you would pay on an additional amount of income given your current income level. Basically, it gets higher as your taxable income gets higher.

In the example we have been looking at, your marginal tax rate was 38.28 percent because you owed an extra $3,828.17 on an addition of $10,000 of taxable income.

The program will show that the $30,000 employee who gets an increase to $40,000 will owe an additional $2,018.05 in tax – that is, a marginal tax rate of 20.18 percent ($2,018.05/$10,000).

But just one minute. This employee will also owe $495 more in CPP and $188 more in EI deductions, so the total tax/CPP/EI bill goes from $5,625.12 (tax of $3,576.12, CPP of $1,485, and EI of $564) to $8,326.17 (tax of $5,594.17, CPP of $1,980, and EI of $752). That is a total increase of $2,701.05 – about 27 percent. While not part of the marginal tax rate, the CPP and EI effect of salary increases on lower-income individuals can be significant.

Marginal tax rates are a powerful thing and the main key to getting your family's total tax bill under control. Table 4.2 will help me explain how important this concept can be to reducing the taxes you pay. It shows the combined federal and Ontario income tax rates for 2014, assuming only the basic personal exemption:

TABLE 4.2 Combined Federal and Ontario Income Tax Rates for 2014 Assuming Only the Basic Personal Exemption

Lower Limit	Upper Limit	Basic Tax	Rate on Excess
$0	$11,138	$0	0.00%
$11,139	$14,086	$0	15.00%
$14,087	$18,502	$442	25.10%
$18,503	$40,120	$1,551	20.05%
$40,121	$43,953	$5,885	24.15%
$43,954	$70,648	$6,811	31.15%
$70,649	$80,242	$15,126	32.98%
$80,243	$83,236	$18,290	35.39%
$83,237	$87,907	$19,350	39.41%
$87,908	$136,270	$21,191	43.41%
$136,271	$514,090	$42,185	46.41%
$514,091	No limit	$217,530	49.53%

Look at the difference in the marginal tax rate, or *rate on excess*. For someone in the second-highest bracket (earning between $136,271 and $514,090 a year), it's 46.41 percent. That means that if this person got a bonus of $10,000, $4,641 would go to the tax department and only $5,359 would be left.

For someone who has no other income, the first $11,138 is tax-free because that's the amount of the basic personal exemption – the marginal tax rate up to that amount is zero. If, for example, a couple with one in the second-highest bracket and the other in the lowest, could shift $10,000 in income from the higher to the lower, they would save $4,641 in tax. This is called *income splitting*, and it's the key to saving taxes.

In the next section, we'll look at income splitting and variations on this simple tax strategy that could save you money. I am not talking about complex trust structures or offshore investing. Just basic moves that many Canadians don't know about or aren't taking advantage of.

PENSION INCOME SPLITTING

The pension income splitting rules could save you thousands of dollars in tax every year – painlessly. Let's discuss how the rules work.

Since 2007, you have been allowed to transfer up to 50 percent of your "eligible pension income" to your spouse or common-law partner.

Income that qualifies for pension splitting depends on the recipient's age. Here's what qualifies, depending on how old you are:

Recipients under age 65:

- Pension income from a registered pension plan (RPP) – for example, pensions from an employer-sponsored defined benefit (DB) or defined contribution (DC) plan
- Certain other payments received as a result of the death of a spouse or common-law partner (e.g., a survivor pension annuity)

Recipients age 65 and older:

- Both payments described above
- Annuity payments from an RRSP
- RRIF withdrawals or withdrawals from RRIFs subject to federal of provincial locked-in legislation, such as life income funds (LIFs) and LRIFs
- Certain amounts received under a retirement compensation arrangement

Also note that eligible pension income amounts also qualify for the $2,000 federal pension income amount, which is a nonrefundable tax credit.

In other words, if you are sixty-five years of age or older, all your pension income is eligible for the transfer. If you are not sixty-five at the end of the year, only your income eligible for the pension income credit is eligible for pension splitting.

The reason that the government limits the requirements for RRSP annuity, RRIF, and LRIF income to those aged sixty-five and over is to target pension splitting and the pension income credit to retired people.

You have much less control over the timing of registered pension plan payments than you do over the amount and timing of withdrawals under RRSPs, RRIFs, and LRIFs. Without the age sixty-five rule, people who aren't retired could gain tax advantages through income splitting well before age sixty-five. Pensioners who receive RPP income generally have little say in the timing of their pension payments, since they usually only begin to receive payments after they retire.

What You Can't Split

Note that pension income for splitting purposes does not include Old Age Security (OAS) benefits, CPP or QPP benefits, death benefits, retiring allowances, RRSP withdrawals (other than annuity payments), or payments out of a Retirement Compensation Arrangement (RCA), salary deferral arrangement, or employee benefit plan.

A foreign pension annuity may qualify for income splitting, but not the portion that is tax exempt due to a tax treaty with the foreign country. Income from a US Individual Retirement Account (IRA) also does not qualify.

How to Split Pension Income

To split your pension income, both you and your spouse or common-law partner will have to make a joint election by completing form T1032 – Joint Election to Split Pension Income. You'll need to file the form with the tax return for the year the pension income is being split, and you'll need to file it on time. The due dates are April 30 of the next year for regular returns, or June 15 if you are self-employed. CRA states that under certain circumstances, you may make a late or amended election, or revoke an original election if the application is made on or before the day that is three calendar years after the filing due date for the year the election applies. So if you have missed a pension-splitting opportunity, it might still be possible to apply for it.

If income tax has been withheld from the pension income, remember to allocate the tax withheld in the same ratio that you reported the pension income.

You have to make the pension income-splitting election on an annual basis. In other words, your decision for one year will not carry forward to the next automatically. Each year you'll need to decide how much of your eligible pension income (if any) you want to split.

To be eligible, you and your spouse or common-law partner must be living together and be residents of Canada at the end of the year or at the date of death of one of you if that happened during the year.

If you and your spouse or common-law partner are living separately at the end of the year due to a breakdown of the relationship, which has lasted for at least ninety days, no transfer is permitted.

If you married or commenced living common-law during the year or if your spouse or common-law partner died during the year, you must pro-rate the amount eligible for transfer by the number of months the relationship existed. The month the relationship began or your spouse or common-law partner died counts as a full month. The number of months the relationship existed is divided by twelve to get the percentage you can transfer.

The transferor deducts the elected split-pension amount on line 210 of his or her income tax return and the transferee spouse or common-law partner adds the same amount to his or her income on line 116 of his or her return.

Benefits of Splitting Pension Income

There are four main benefits to splitting pension income.

Advantage #1 - Less Tax

As you know, if the transferee spouse or common-law partner is in a lower marginal tax bracket at the time of the transfer, as a couple your combined tax will be lower. That's because the taxable income of the higher tax bracket spouse will be decreased and the taxable income of the lower tax bracket spouse will be increased.

If you are doing your own calculations to optimize the transfer, the benefits of using a computer-based program speak for themselves, unless you like doing dozens of manual calculations!

Advantage #2 - The $2,000 Pension Credit

If the transferee spouse is sixty-five or over at the end of the taxation year for which you are splitting pension income, the transferee may include the transferred income along with any other eligible pension income in claiming the $2,000 pension income credit.

Therefore, if your spouse or common-law partner is not already eligible to utilize his or her $2,000 pension credit, he or she will be able to reduce the tax bill. This may result in a combined credit of $4,000 instead of $2,000, as you both make the claim.

If the transferee spouse or common-law partner is not yet sixty-five at the end of the tax year, he or she may still claim the amount of qualified pension income that is transferred. In this case, the eligible pension income would include the transferor's private pension or annuity income plus certain amounts received as a result of the death of his or her former spouse or common-law partner. Note that in this situation, the transferor's RRSP, RRIF, or DPSP income does not qualify.

Advantage #3 - Increasing OAS Benefits

Depending on your current net income levels, diverting pension income to your spouse or common-law partner could increase your OAS benefit by reducing the amount of the OAS clawback.

The maximum OAS benefit for 2014 is $6,677, but it is reduced (or clawed back) by 15 percent of net income in excess of $71,592. The entire amount of OAS is clawed back when your net income reaches $116,103, because 15 percent of $116,103 less $71,592 equals $6,677, the whole OAS pension.

So if your net income exceeded $71,592 in 2014 and you can reduce your net income by allocating some of your pension income to your spouse or common-law partner, you might reduce the amount of OAS that would otherwise have been clawed back when you filed your 2014 tax return. It should be noted that if the splitting results in your spouse or common-law partner's net income being above $71,592, his or her OAS benefit may be reduced.

Advantage #4 - Increasing Other Credits

It is important to note that it is possible for a low-income spouse or common-law partner to transfer unused nonrefundable tax credits including age, pension, eligible dependent, and tuition/education/textbook amounts to his or her higher-income spouse or common-law partner. To the extent that the lower-income spouse had other nonrefundable and nontransferrable amounts eligible that can be used to offset the transferred pension income, there would be a net tax savings.

Also, the transferor may be able to increase some other nonrefundable credits like the age amount, which would have been reduced by his or her higher income before the transfer.

How Much Pension Income to Transfer

If you and your spouse or common-law partner are in the same income tax bracket and are both using the full $2,000 pension nonrefundable tax credit, there is probably no benefit to transferring any pension income.

If, however, one of you is in a higher income tax bracket, it's probably best to transfer an amount to bring your spouse or common-law partner up to the amount of income where your tax bracket starts. If he or she is in an even lower tax bracket, the maximum 50 percent is probably the answer.

Even if you are both in the same income tax bracket, it probably makes sense to transfer at least enough pension income so your spouse or common-law partner can fully utilize the $2,000 pension credit, assuming the pension income transferred is eligible for credit in his or her hands if he or she is under sixty-five.

How to Claim the Pension Income Amount

If you and your spouse or common-law partner elected to split your eligible pension income, follow the instructions at step 4 on form T1032 – Joint Election to Split Pension Income, to calculate the amount to enter on line 314 of your and your spouse's or common-law partner's Schedule 1. This is the pension income amount. Each of you will be able to claim the lesser of $2,000 or the amount of your eligible pension income, after excluding amounts allocated to your spouse or common-law partner.

Spousal RRSPs: Still a Useful Tool

With the rules allowing you to split RRSP annuity and RRIF income, are spousal RRSPs still useful? In a word: yes.

A spousal (or common-law partner) RRSP is a plan in which one spouse or common-law partner has contributed to an RRSP and the other spouse or common-law partner is the owner or annuitant. It is often used by couples for post-retirement income-splitting purposes, as funds are withdrawn and taxed in the hands of the annuitant spouse rather than the contributor spouse. If the annuitant spouse is in a lower tax bracket than the contributor spouse at the time of the withdrawal, there can be a reduction of the couple's tax bill.

The amount you can contribute to a spousal RRSP is determined by the contributor's RRSP limits, not the annuitant's. In other words, it doesn't matter if your spouse or common-law partner does not work and therefore has no RRSP room – it's your room that counts.

Contributions to a spousal plan become the property of your spouse or common-law partner; however, there is one important catch to be aware of. If funds are withdrawn within three taxation years of *any* contribution to the plan, the withdrawal will be reportable by the contributor spouse or partner, effectively undoing the strategy.

Advantage #1 – Splitting Income Under Age Sixty-Five

Under the pension-splitting rules, if you are under sixty-five, eligible pension income includes payments from an RPP, but generally not amounts paid from an RRSP or RRIF. Therefore, anyone who wishes to retire before age sixty-five who does not have an RPP should still consider the use of a spousal RRSP to allow the withdrawals to be taxed in a lower income spouse or common-law partner's hands without having to wait until age sixty-five.

If you have determined that you don't need the maximum you could put into an RRSP to fund your retirement, there is another way to split income well before retirement. A high-income spouse could make spousal RRSP contributions and get the tax refund at the high marginal tax rate. After waiting the required three years, the spouse or common-law partner could withdraw the amount and pay the lower amount of tax. This essentially shifts income from a high bracket to a low bracket over three-year intervals.

Advantage #2 – Splitting More than 50 Percent

It may make sense for a couple to transfer more than the 50 percent allowed under the pension-splitting rules. For example, a very high income person with a spouse or common-law partner who does not work may wish to transfer up to 100 percent of his or her RRSP to the nonworking spouse or common-law partner.

This is possible with a spousal RRSP, but not with regular pension splitting.

Advantage #3 – Contributors over Age Seventy-One

After you turn seventy-one, you'll have converted your RRSP to an RRIF (or annuity) as required. You can, however, continue to contribute to a spousal RRSP if you have RRSP contribution room and your spouse or common-law partner is under age seventy-two.

In fact, if you continue working into your seventies, you may still be generating "earned income" for RRSP purposes and thus be able to contribute to a spousal RRSP, as long as your spouse or common-law partner is under age seventy-two.

It should also be noted that even if you aren't working but own a rental property, net rental income from a rental property also qualifies as earned income for purposes of calculating eligible RRSP contribution room.

Advantage #4 – RRSP Home Buyers' Plan Withdrawals

An RRSP Home Buyer's Plan (HBP) allows new home buyers to withdraw up to $25,000 from their RRSPs for the down payment on a new home. This allows people with no other savings than their RRSPs to get into a home.

If one spouse is working and the other is not, the working spouse could contribute $25,000 to his or her own RRSP and $25,000 to a spousal RRSP over the years, allowing $25,000 each, or $50,000 to be withdrawn under the HBP.

Advantage #5 – RRSP Deduction upon Death

If an individual dies with unused RRSP contribution room available, the executor of the deceased's will can make an RRSP contribution to a surviving spouse or common-law partner's spousal RRSP and get an RRSP deduction on the deceased's final tax return.

SELF-EMPLOYMENT – KING OF THE INCOME SPLITTERS

The problem with standard employment is that you don't have the flexibility to decide whose tax return the income goes on. You do the work, you get paid, your T4 employment slip comes in your name, and you pay tax on the income.

The senior executive can't simply call the payroll department and say, "Can you please put $10,000 of my income on a separate T4 for my spouse?"

Want to save tax? Self-employment is worth a look.

The reason for this is that you are allowed to pay reasonable salaries to a spouse as well as children who contribute to your business. But the key here is to follow the rules. There has to be legitimate work being done. For example, CRA may ask you to prove that you would have paid an unrelated person the same amount for the services rendered. It may even be a good idea to go so far as to keep time sheets for the work done. There also needs to be a flow of funds to your spouse or children's separate bank accounts as well as regular payroll deductions and remittances – you can't simply take the salary off your income tax return and add it to theirs.

However, if you have a small business, someone has to create invoices, pay taxes, collect payments, go to the bank and post office, pick up supplies, and keep things clean. It doesn't have to be you – you could hire your spouse or child as an employee and pay the employee a reasonable salary for these administrative and maintenance tasks.

Let's take a look at an example. How much further ahead would a couple in their own business be compared to an executive who made the same amount of money?

Let's assume the executive had a gross salary of $130,000 in Ontario in 2014. Here's what his tax return would show (see Table 4.3).

TABLE 4.3 Tax Return of an Executive with a Gross Salary of $130,000

One Executive	
Gross income	$130,000.00
Federal income tax	$23,110.80
Ontario income tax	$13,675.02
Total taxes	$36,785.82
CPP deduction	$2,425.50
EI deduction	$913.67
Total taxes, CPP and EI	$40,124.99
Net amount	$89,875.01

Note that I have assumed nonrefundable tax credit claim codes of $22,276 federally and $19,340 for Ontario to incorporate the claim for a spouse with no income.

If the executive was instead self-employed and could split the income with a spouse and report $90,000 and $40,000 on separate income tax returns, this is the result (see Table 4.4).

TABLE 4.4 Tax Return of a Self-Employed Executive with Gross Income Reported on Separate Income Tax Returns

	Self-Employment		
	Spouse 1	Spouse 2	Combined
Gross income	$90,000.00	$40,000.00	$130,000.00
Federal income tax	$13,985.84	$3,566.27	$17,552.11
Ontario income tax	$7,099.34	$1,752.90	$8,852.24
Total taxes	$21,085.18	$5,319.17	$26,404.35
CPP deduction	$2,425.50	$1,980.00	$4,405.50
CPP deduction (self-employed)	$2,425.50	$1,980.00	$4,405.50
EI deduction	$0.00	$0.00	$0.00
Total taxes, CPP and EI	$25,936.18	$9,279.17	$35,215.35
Net amount	$64,063.82	$30,720.83	$94,784.65

Note that the combined taxes decline from $36,785.82 to $26,404.35. That's a significant savings of $10,381.47.

But, as with most things in personal finance, there are a few more issues that need to be noted.

First of all, when you are self-employed, you don't have to pay into the EI system. The flip side of that coin is that if you go out of business you do not get to claim EI benefits.

CPP is a different story. Self-employed people have to make CPP contributions and, since there is no employer, they also have to pay the amount that the employer otherwise would have. That doubles the amount that each of the spouses has to pay. One of the amounts is claimed as a nonrefundable tax credit and the other can be deducted from the self-employed person's taxable income. These CPP deductions have been taken into account in Table 4.4.

Now don't take this as advice to quit your high-paying job because you don't like the tax bill – that would be nuts. Take it under consideration for the future. Self-employment income is easier to split than salary. If it makes sense in your case, you should consider it seriously.

But I Don't Know Anything About Being Self-Employed

Well maybe not, but given the financial environment we live in currently, you would be wise to start educating yourself about self-employment.

Think about it. Companies worldwide are being forced to cut costs any way they can. Mergers and acquisitions, government buyouts, or layoffs are being discussed in the majority of boardrooms at this very moment. Face it: There is no more job security. Jobs for life are a thing of the past.

All is not lost, however. Companies still need people to do the work, even after layoffs. Going back into the workforce as a consultant is going to be a more and more common theme in the years to come.

Unfortunately, many people are going to be forced into this against their will. Think of a fifty-eight-year-old senior manager forced to retire from a company he has been with for thirty years. Where is he going to find a job in his field? He will probably be at a high pay level, and there will be much younger/cheaper alternatives available to the companies at which he would be applying for a job.

On the other hand, he would have plenty of experience, and if he were to seek contract assignments, he would be a lot cheaper than a full-time employee because of the cost of benefits. That's key to your pitch to potential clients: They won't have to pay for your CPP, EI, Employer Health Tax, pensions, a health plan, and workers' compensation, as well as potential severance payments.

Self-Employment Does Not Have to Be Complicated

Many people are scared of self-employment, but you don't have to be. In its simplest form, it can be one self-motivated person operating out of his or her home.

Here are some basic facts that should help to put your mind at ease:

- **The name.** If you operate under your own name (e.g., Jane Smith, Consultant), you don't even need to register the business name. Just put that at the top of your letterhead and you are set to go.
- **Goods and services tax (GST) or harmonized sales tax (HST).** Until you bill more than $30,000 in a single year you don't need to register for or start collecting the GST/HST.
- **Bank account.** If you operate under your own name, you can make deposits to a personal bank account in your name. No need to open up a business account with higher bank fees.
- **Bookkeeping.** You don't need to buy a bookkeeping software package at first if you don't want to. Just keep track of all of your business-related expenses so you can deduct them from your income.

CONCLUSION

There you have it – the information and tools you'll need to painlessly reduce two of the biggest expenses you'll probably ever have – interest and taxes.

Now let's delve into the next area – why it may be best to start your RRSP later in life.

5

FORGET RRSPS UNTIL YOUR DEBT IS PAID OFF (THE OPPORTUNITY ZONE)

Yes, that's what I said, and yes, it goes against traditional retirement planning advice. You know, the "start early – the earlier the better" and "pay yourself first" type of advice. The truth is that it may really be better to start late.

When you work through the numbers and consider the risks involved with investing in the stock market while you are still in debt, you may come to the same conclusion I have: you are much better off to focus on buying a home and paying off all debt, including the home mortgage, before you start to save for retirement.

PRETEND THE STOCK MARKET DOES NOT EXIST

I think a strong case can be made to ignore the stock market altogether when it comes to saving for retirement. The risk of stock market disaster is simply too great. This is especially true if you start saving late, because there is less time to recover from a stock market crash. So how do you ignore the stock market? Pretend it doesn't even exist.

That's correct – every dollar you invest from now on goes into 100% no-risk government-guaranteed fixed-income GICs.

THE RRSP FALLACY

During our spending years when we are in debt, they ask us to make RRSP contributions, don't they? In fact, they want us to start as early as possible. You know, to realize the benefits of "compounding."

The truth is that these clever word plays make the product-pushers rich ... and you poor.

How so? Well since we are in debt, the only way we can make those RRSP contributions is by borrowing to do it. In other words, if you take $1,000 from your chequing account to make an RRSP contribution, you are borrowing to do it at the highest interest rate you have because that $1,000 could have otherwise gone to reduce your highest interest debt. All that debt you have is compounding too – against you. It is compounding to the benefit of the financial institution that extended the loan to you.

Here's a simple example. Tom has $10,000 of credit card debt at an interest rate of 20% a year. He has a marginal tax rate of 40% (each additional dollar he earns he pays $0.40 in tax and for each dollar he contributes to an RRSP he gets a $0.40 refund). I'll assume the RRSP contribution is made on January 1 and grows at 5% a year and that the earnings are added to the RRSP account on December 31. I'll also assume any credit card interest is paid before the last day of the year. See Tables 5.1 and 5.2.

TABLE 5.1   Case 1 – RRSP Contribution (Year 1)

	January 1, Year 1	Cash In (Out) During Year	December 31, Year 1
RRSP Balance	$0		$10,500
RRSP Contribution		($10,000)	
RRSP Tax Refund		$4,000	
Credit Card Balance	($10,000)		($10,000)
Pay Down Credit Card		$0	
Credit Card Interest Expense		($2,000)	
Bank Balance	$14,000	($8,000)	$6,000
Net worth	$4,000		$6,500

TABLE 5.2   Case 2 – Pay Down Credit Card (Year 1)

	January 1, Year 1	Cash In (Out) During Year	December 31, Year 1
RRSP Balance	$0	$0	$0
RRSP Contribution		$0	
RRSP Tax Refund		$0	
Credit Card Balance	($10,000)		$0
Pay Down Credit Card		($10,000)	
Credit Card Interest Expense		$0	
Bank Balance	$14,000	($10,000)	$4,000
Net Worth	$4,000		$4,000

At first glance it appears the RRSP is the way to go. Your after-tax cash outflow during the year is only $8,000 in case 1 versus $10,000 in case 2.

Your net worth also is higher – $6,500 versus $4,000 under case 2. But the RRSP chart ignores one important thing – taxes. It's showing what the RRSP is worth before it is cashed-in. If the RRSP was cashed in and the 40% tax bill paid, the RRSP would give only $6,300 in cash ($10,500 less 40%). The net worth after year 1 would then be only $2,300, which is lower than case 2

Stop here at your peril, as there is even more to the story than that. Let's look at year 2. See Tables 5.3 and 5.4:

TABLE 5.3   Case 1 – RRSP Contribution (Year 2)

	January 1, Year 2	Cash In (Out) During Year	December 31, Year 2
RRSP Balance	$10,500		$11,025
RRSP Contribution		$0	
RRSP Tax Refund		$0	
Credit Card Balance	($10,000)		($10,000)
Pay Down Credit Card		$0	
Credit Card Interest Expense		($2,000)	
Bank Balance	$6,000	($2,000)	$4,000
Net Worth	$6,500		$5,025

TABLE 5.4   Case 2 – Pay Down Credit Card (Year 2)

	January 1, Year 2	Cash In (Out) During Year	December 31, Year 2
RRSP Balance	$0	$0	$0
RRSP Contribution		$0	
RRSP Tax Refund		$0	
Credit Card Balance	$0		$0
Pay Down Credit Card		$0	
Credit Card Interest Expense		$0	
Bank Balance	$4,000		$4,000
Net Worth	$4,000	$0	$4,000

Can you see another problem with the RRSP strategy? Each and every year after year 1, in this case, $2,000 is continuing to flow out to the credit card company while your RRSP grows at only 5%. Look at the net worth of the RRSP strategy after year 1 and compare it to year 2. It has declined by $1,475 from $6,500 to $5,025. That's because $2,000 in interest has gone to the credit card company while the RRSP has grown by only $525. Meanwhile the pay down credit card net worth has remained at $4,000.

On an after-tax basis, the RRSP strategy net worth after year 2 would only be $615 since the $11,025 RRSP would be cashed in and would lose 40%, $4,410, to taxes.

Say Tom carries his credit card debt from year to year. Assuming he only pays the interest each year, and doesn't put anything else on his card, he would have paid $10,000 in interest in five years. But what if he doesn't have the cash to pay the interest? How much total interest would he have paid after five years? Not just $10,000, because the interest keeps adding to the amount owing and the 20% is applied to the increasing amount. This is compounding working against him. After five years his credit card balance would be $24,883. He would have been charged $14,883 in total interest. Either way, that's a huge amount of cash going down the drain.

That's the RRSP fallacy. Each and every year you are in debt, real cash is being drained from your bank account. Even if it's not credit card debt at 20%, in many cases it's at something higher than the actual return you are getting on your RRSP. But of course, they don't tell you what you're making on your RRSP do they? Could it be 5%, 8%, 10%? For many people the sad reality is that after fees, the answer is much lower than they had hoped.

The conclusion is simple: if you've got credit card debt, forget about making an RRSP contribution until the debt is gone.

COMPOUND THIS

The next time your mutual fund salesperson uses the "benefits of compounding" argument to try to convince you to hand over more hard-earned cash for him to play with, remind him that you still have debt and therefore compounding is eating away at you.

Yes, I agree you should realize the benefits of compounding, but do it simply with no risk. That is, by paying off all debt, including your house mortgage, before investing another dime in your RRSP.

THE TAX TURBO-CHARGED RRSP

One of the main advantages of a delayed RRSP strategy is taxes. This is because since you are debt free, you'll have a significant amount of cash to make a large RRSP contribution and that contribution will lead to a large tax refund because you'll probably be in your peak earnings years at the highest tax bracket you'll ever be in. Each year's refund will be immediately reinvested in your RRSP, leading to significantly increased contributions.

Instead of trying to benefit from compounding that requires you to save for decades, use the benefit of taxes to get where you'd like to be without risk. Let's dig a bit deeper, shall we?

A WORD ABOUT YOUR RRSP LIMIT

First and foremost, it is important to note that all the RRSP room you built up during the early years where you were making earned income for RRSP purposes but not making RRSP contributions carries forward. In other words, if you were eligible to contribute say $15,000 each year for ten years, and you didn't, after the ten-year period you would have accumulated $150,000 of RRSP contribution room.

The amount you have accumulated is shown on your annual Notice of Assessment that the federal government mails you after reviewing your income tax return each year. It's usually shown at the bottom of one of the pages in a box titled "RRSP/PRPP Deduction Limit Statement" and it looks like this (see Figure 5.1):

FIGURE 5.1   RRSP/PRPP Deduction Limit Statement - 2014

Date	Name	Social insurance no.	Tax year	Tax centre
May 12, 2014	PAT SMITH	111 222 333	2013	Sudbury ON P3A 5C1

Your 2014 RRSP/PRPP Deduction Limit Statement
The back of this notice contains important information. Amounts marked with an asterisk (*) cannot be less than zero.

RRSP/PRPP deduction limit for 2013		$20,000
Minus: Employer's PRPP contributions for 2013		$0
Minus: Allowable RRSP/PRPP contributions deducted for 2013		$12,000
Unused RRSP/PRPP deduction limit at the end of 2013		$8,000
Plus: 18% of 2013 earned income of $50,000 = (max. $24,270).	$9,000	
Minus: 2013 pension adjustment	$0	$9,000 *
		$17,000
Minus: 2014 net past service pension adjustment		$0
Plus: 2014 pension adjustment reversal		$0
Your **RRSP/PRPP deduction limit for 2014**		$17,000 *(A)

You have $0 **(B)** of **unused RRSP/PRPP contributions** available for 2014. If this amount is more than amount **(A)** above, you may have to pay a tax on the excess contributions.

Look at the bottom figure **(A)**. That's the key to the Tax Turbo-Charged RRSP. Don't worry that it is building up year after year; it's RRSP room that you'll use later.

Note that PRPP stands for Pooled Registered Pension Plan. It is a retirement savings option that started in 2013 for individuals including those who are self-employed that allows members to benefit from lower administration costs from participating in a large, pooled pension plan. It is portable and moves with you from job to job and is similar to an RRSP.

DO YOU TRUST THE STOCK MARKET?

But hold on a minute. We've just barely recovered from 2008, and this has shown the major weakness of the traditional RRSP strategy of starting early and trusting the stock market: in a matter of months your whole plan could be decimated and it could take years to recover.

The crash of 2008 has also had a large impact on the often-quoted 8% to 10% average rate of return that the Canadian stock market has generated over the long term. Let's look at that.

On June 30, 1983 the S&P/TSX Composite Index was 2,447. On June 18, 2008 it peaked at 15,073. During that twenty-five year time span the average annual rate of return was 7.5%. On July 31, 2014 it was 15,446. Twenty-five years before that on July 31, 1989 it was 3,971. The twenty-five year average annual rate of return for this period had declined to only 5.6%.

I have used a 5% average rate of return on many of the examples in this book. Based on what has just happened, that could even be difficult to achieve. Besides the possibility of lower returns in the future, there are two factors that may draw average equity-based portfolios down to rates available with GICs.

The two reasons are fees and the need to diversify to reduce risk. Let me explain.

Those Ugly Fees

The main reason I have assumed a 5% rate of return throughout this book is because I am factoring in fees. In other words, if the stock market (equities) makes 7% a year during your investing horizon, and you use a typical Canadian equity mutual fund to try and get that return, you'll give up about 2% of that return in fees through the management expenses of that fund. That leaves you with only a 5% return.

The new reality is that stock market returns may only be around 5% going forward. Take off fees and you'll only get 3%.

Don't Put All Your Eggs in One Basket

But having 100% in equities is an extremely risky strategy. As we have just seen you could lose almost 50% of your nest egg in a matter of months. That's why even many mutual fund sales people recommend that you diversify your asset mix. That means you should include a safe fixed-income component.

Say you decide to leave 65% of your portfolio in equity mutual funds at 5% return a year and 35% of your portfolio in safe GICs at 3% return a year. Your weighted average rate of return is as follows:

$$= (5\% \times 65\%) + (3\% \times 35\%)$$
$$= 4.3\%$$

Maybe even 5% is too high to use as an average expected rate of return for a well-balanced portfolio.

CONCLUSION

No one is sure whether the next twenty, thirty or fifty years will return the same results as the market has over the last twenty, thirty or fifty – a period of significant real economic growth after World War II.

What happens if the future is not so rosy?

Unfortunately the answer is not pretty. If you believe you can earn 5% a year on average after fees in your RRSP over the time you have left to retirement, and you actually do make 5%, your plan may work.

The problem is, will you actually realize that rate? What used to be an easily achievable goal of 5% a year now seems unlikely. Remember, it took six years from 2008 to get back to the amount originally invested – that's a 0% rate of return!

Even if the future brings us back to the level of prosperity that our parents enjoyed, you may be better off forgetting the whole stock market thing and leaving it to the large financial institutions who know how it works like the back of their hand.

For me, I'd rather not spend the rest of my life worrying about what the stock market might do. I'd rather sleep at night knowing that it makes absolutely no difference to me or my family.

6

YOU MAY NOT NEED AN INVESTMENT ADVISOR

Don't get me wrong here – I strongly recommend that you use an investment advisor.

There are significant advantages to having a good one working for you including:

- **It takes time.** How many spare hours do you have each day to devote to your personal finances? Yeah, that's what I thought. We are all busy and having someone else doing the work for us simply makes sense if we are unlikely to spend the time ourselves.
- **Expertise is needed.** The more investment products and financial schemes you get involved in, the more you'll need to know about how they work. Good investment advisors will spend much of their daily working life researching the many products and options available, and using their experience and skills to make decisions. Will you be able to to the same?
- **Emotion is your enemy.** If you do all your own investing you'll probably find that, like many humans, greed and fear often get in the way of good investing habits. For example, if you were brilliant enough to pick a stock that doubled in price in one

year, when do you pull the trigger and sell it? Many people suffer large financial losses waiting too long to sell a winner or selling a loser before it rebounds.

There are many good, qualified investment advisors out there and you should spend the time and effort to try and find one.

The problem is they are hard to find. Many people use their friends, relatives or even neighbours. That can be a recipe for disaster.

MY STORY

I'd like to tell you my story not because I am a particularly great investor or so that you will follow what I did. I'd like to tell you because I think it has some important lessons and has actual numbers that really happened.

I started making RRSP contributions in February 1991 when I was thirty-two years old. Just like many of you I started with the big bank that my parents had always used and invested in the bank's balanced equity mutual funds. I did this again in 1992.

In 1993, I listened to the siren call of the new mutual fund companies that were starting to emerge. Boy, they had great advertising! I bought into my first one that year.

In 1994, I was introduced to a new tax savings opportunity – Labour-Sponsored Investment Funds (LSIFs). At the time you could invest up to $5,000 a year and get a 20% federal and a 20% Ontario tax credit, for $2,000 refund. That sounded good to me. I bought into one.

The lure of the tax refund was so strong that I continued to buy LSIFs in 1995 and 1996.

It was also at this time that I ran into the brother of a friend of mine who happened to work at a big brokerage firm. Since I was busy at work and investments seemed to be getting more and more complicated, I decided to transfer my self-directed holdings at several different banks and mutual fund companies to him.

From 1997 until 2002, I religiously drank the Kool-Aid of traditional retirement advice and made RRSP contributions through thick and thin.

Here is a summary of the contributions I made, including the LSIF tax refunds I received. Table 6.1

TABLE 6.1 RRSP Contributions from 2/28/91 to 3/1/2002

Date Contributed	Amount Contributed	LSIF Refund	Net Amount Contributed	Invested With
2/28/1991	4,000.00	0.00	4,000.00	BANK Balanced Equity Fund
2/28/1992	4,000.00	0.00	4,000.00	BANK Balanced Equity Fund
2/28/1993	6,000.00	0.00	6,000.00	MUTUAL FUND CO. #1
2/28/1994	5,177.50	2,000.00	3,177.50	MUTUAL FUND CO. #2
2/28/1995	5,000.00	2,000.00	3,0000.00	LSIF
2/28/1996	5,000.00	1,050.00	3,950.00	LSIF
2/28/1997	5,000.00	1,050.00	3,950.00	BROKER ($3,500 LSIF #1)
2/28/1998	5,000.00	1,500.00	3,500.00	BROKER ($3,500 LSIF #2)
7/31/1998	7,500.00		7,500.00	BROKER
2/28/1999	8,000.00	1,500.00	6,500.00	BROKER ($5,000 LSIF #3)
2/28/2000	10,000.00	1,500.00	8,500.00	BROKER ($5,000 LSIF #4)
2/28/2001	12,000.00	0.00	12,000.00	BROKER ($5,000 LSIF #5)
3/1/2002	5,000.00	0.00	5,000.00	BROKER
TOTALS	**81,677.50**	**10,600.00**	**71,077.50**	

But there was a problem. In fact, there was more than one problem.

First of all, I never knew how well the investments were doing. I'd get statements showing "Book Value" and the month-end market value, but not the most important figure of all – my personal rate of return!

Whenever I asked for it, I got a convoluted answer about how complicated it was to compute. Sometimes I'd get a handwritten summary of estimated returns. In fact, whenever I had a conversation with this guy, it went on so long I had to say I had a meeting just to get off the phone.

That's when, by going over old tax returns, I made the summary you see above. I wanted to see how well I was doing since I started.

Now, to be fair, this guy inherited the balanced equity funds, and a couple of mutual funds and LSIFs that I had purchased from 1991 to 1996, but when I compared the actual contributions above to the market value of the entire portfolio on June 30, 2004, I got a value of $89,092.56. What was my rate of return during the period?

At this time I was writing my first book, *Smoke and Mirrors*, and I created a spreadsheet that comes with it called the "Personal Rate of Return Calculator." It computes your personal rate of return for any period of time. I used the PRR calculator and was surprised to find out that even after factoring in the LSIF tax refunds, that my actual personal rate of return was only 3.28% a year.

To get the real rate of return you'd have to ignore the income tax refunds because they were funded by the government and had nothing to do with the return on the investments themselves. The real rate of return without the tax refunds was only 1.26%.

Here's where it get interesting. During the same period March 1991 to June 2004, the S&P/TSX Composite Index rose to 8,398 from 3,495 – an average annual rate of return of 6.97%. I wasn't 100% in equities so I didn't expect to match that, but I was significantly invested in the stock market to the tune of over 75%. Shouldn't I have expected a return of more than 1% or so?

What I Did Next

I knew I was not getting the results I desired or the service I needed, but there was a problem. I didn't want to take full responsibility for my own investing, especially since I was stuck in a lot of stuff that was not transparent and included those LSIFs.

So I stayed with the original advisor and decided to stop making RRSP contributions.

A few years later I was lucky enough to come across an advisor who was a Chartered Professional Accountant (CPA) like me and even worked at the same CPA firm that I did. He was the author of several books on investing and I attended a course he taught at the Chartered Professional Accountants of Ontario (CPAO). We got to know each other and he offered to do a free portfolio review of my accounts.

The result was a large spreadsheet listing each investment, the category it was in (fixed income, Canadian equity, foreign equity, LSIF etc.), the DSC fee to get out of each investment, the date when each would be free from a DSC, and the date each LSIF would be free from having to pay back the income tax refund.

The results clearly showed I was more than 80% high risk and that I could get out of a significant number of investments DSC free.

Together we began the slow process of getting out of the "dog" mutual funds and getting to the safety of GICs and government bonds.

This took place over the years, to the point where the entire portfolio structure was reversed so that as of the middle of 2008, 80% was fixed income and only 20% was exposed to the stock market. As a result, the fall of 2008 was not as devastating to me as to others.

WHAT TO LOOK FOR IN AN INVESTMENT ADVISOR

When selecting an investment advisor, you should obviously look for someone who is well-educated and has qualifications directly related to personal finances. I would also suggest that you look for someone with experience in up and down markets. Trusting your family's nest egg to a hotshot twenty-five-year-old is courting disaster.

Beyond that, I would pay particular attention to what the potential advisor has to say in your first few face-to-face meetings. Does he or she:

- Listen to your questions and provide simple answers?
- Ask about all the other things in your life, like your housing situation, debt levels and plans for retirement, or does he just zero in on your investments?
- Seem overly friendly and want to chat about your kids, hobbies and other interests? Many advisors are great at emotional selling, but you don't want to *be sold* – you want to buy some good independent expertise.

Then ask what he or she thinks of Canada's retirement system – the CPP and OAS pension. Those who say it's at risk of not surviving may be trying to scare you into investing more with them.

FOR THOSE WHO HAVE A LOUSY ADVISOR

You probably already know if you've got a lousy advisor. The market value of your portfolio seems to go up sometimes but most often it goes down. He doesn't return your phone calls to explain why. Your investment statements show no evidence of how well your investments are doing, and contain confusing and contradictory descriptions for products, such as "monthly income" for high-risk equity stuff. You've therefore got no idea of how much you are exposed to high-risk products – is it 80% when it should be less than 20%?

NO ADVISOR IS BETTER THAN A BAD ONE

The truth is that if you stick to the concepts laid out in this book – avoid disasters, buy a home if you can afford one, pay for an expert to handle your taxes, only invest in what you can understand, and pay off all debt before you retire – you don't need to find that elusive investment advisor that you can trust with your family's future.

Because the plan is so simple, you can do it yourself. It won't keep you up at night.

HENRY'S STORY

I have my own ideas about the usefulness of an investment advisor, but I wanted to get the first-hand experiences of an expert. I wanted to find someone who had been trained in the world of finance and worked in the financial sector for at least thirty years, someone who had experience with his own personal finances and used various investment brokers both at work and personally. This person would also have to believe in the stock market.

I found such a person in a family friend that I'll call Henry. Here is Henry's story in his own words:

HENRY'S STORY
Dear David

You asked me to provide my views on personal financial investing. My views were developed from 30 years in the finance function in the business world after getting my MBA and by the experiences I have had myself with personal investments.

Initially I worked in a manufacturing company with a global "empire" and a Canadian operation (Company #1) which pretended to be independent. Nevertheless the financial training program was excellent and I became heavily involved in the Treasury function. Company #1 was considered to be at the forefront of managing pension investments.

The global Company #1 had done a study which measured the performance of a dozen of the best pension managers in the world. Over a period of ten

---

years these managers had the unfettered discretion to move money between fixed income and equity markets. Not remembering exactly the actual numbers, if in the measurement period the real rate of return on fixed investments was 3% and the real rate of return on equity investments was 5% one would expect the portfolio managers would achieve a return somewhere between 3% and 5%. As it turned out, the best efforts of the collective wisdom of a dozen of the best pension managers who could be retained by a global household-name empire turned in actual returns notably under 3%. Throw a dart at a board with random scattered numbers from 1 to 100. Use the dart landing point to establish the equity/fixed mix at time zero. If you want, at the last minute, reverse the number to fixed income/equity mix. Whichever choice you make, hold that mix and by the end of the period you will beat the average of the managers. As a consequence, by the time I became involved, Company #1 had turned the first corner and managed the fixed income/equity mix itself, leaving the content of the equity portfolio to the outside experts. This experience created Principle #1 in my thinking:

Principle #1: No one can time the markets

In the seventies and early eighties Company #1 focused heavily on relative performance of external managers in the equity markets. Every quarter we prepared charts and packages with comparisons among our 7 or 8 managers – showing actual absolute returns and actual returns versus the stock exchanges and against other managers for annual, four year and four year rolling returns and returns for each manager from the beginning of time. The first portion of most meetings was dedicated to complaints about data inaccuracies. Then the managers would explain the troughs and spikes in their charts. The spikes were usually the results of their unique clever actions (eg. methanol prices rise globally and methanol stocks go up dramatically). Any pension manager holding such stock gets credit. Meanwhile managers without such stock are grilled by the company representatives in reverse rank order. Our goal was to get an answer to the question: "How could you be so stupid to not buy methanol stocks!" We interviewed potential new managers steadily, mostly by their own initiative. They all had certain skills –rarely acquired in any actual industry job, but at hard work in business schools, investment companies and banks where they developed personal skills of magnitude. After several years of this process I learned that the managers really had very little capability of picking stocks successfully to beat other managers or stock market indices. They did their best and kept trying "new approaches" – technical, contrary, value, large cap, small cap and many others. They tried showing unique measuring periods- all performance measurements are so sensitive to starting and ending periods – it was often possible to find some good news in any mess. They brought in their research people from the back room. Some of them had good runs but the inevitability was always there and one major offside decision could get them fired. Mostly they weathered the stormy periods and basked in invisibility in the good periods.

In this period I developed Principle #2 in my thinking:

(continued)

(*continued*)

Principle #2 Today's hero is tomorrow's loser

In the early eighties I moved to Company #2 where I had less involvement with pensions but what I did see was "more of the same" in terms of investment performance . Principles #1 and #2 were re-validated.

Although it has nothing to do with individual personal investing, one of my responsibilities at Company #2 was to obtain approval for the actuarial rate which would determine the pension expense applied against profits. This was like the blind leading the blind. The Corporate sponsors were motivated to maximize profits; therefore a higher rate was more desirable. Meanwhile the experts who could not time anything and were on their way to being heroes or bums added their input generally preferring a low rate – easier target to beat in the future. External auditors grumbled but generally agreed with management.

In the mid nineties I became CFO of a Canadian-based multinational public company – Company #3. By this time I had seen enough and pushed aggressively to move to index funds for the equity portion of the fund. Index funds can duplicate the "averages" quite successfully and accurately. Because there is no opportunity to add value and charge enormous fees, pension investment managers were obviously reluctant to acknowledge the value of index funds.

Principle #3 People on commission cannot be trusted

This principle applies in the investment world as well. You have to understand the priorities of your advisor. Clearly the first priority is himself and his career and what that means for his family. More than likely his second priority is his employer who is very important to our advisor's future; and clearly the third priority is the client.

So, now we have in total an advisor who has no way to time markets or pick stocks effectively. Furthermore his priorities are not totally aligned with yours. He is bright, well educated, and intelligent and you are going to put your financial security in his hands. The best you can hope for is a win/win/win outcome because if anyone doesn't win, the highest probability is that you are the loser – Win/Win/Lose.

Of course they want your repeat business but the primary responsibility of your investment advisor is to get you to buy or sell something – anything. You want my ideas? Your ideas? What the firm recommends? Guess what the firm recommends – paper it issues for its corporate clients is top priority. At the Monday morning Sales meeting the troops are brought in and told this week they have to peddle W shares of X Corporation or $Y million of Z Corporation notes. Step right up troops. The more you take on the more you impress your boss and your cohorts in the room. You know you will be able to stuff it into accounts of the unwary or overly trusting clients.

Henry's Personal Investments

With the above background, here is what happened with one of our portfolios. It is non-registered, was initially established as an investment portfolio and latterly as a vehicle to generate income. The portfolio was started with $500,000 in late 1994 and early 1995 and was given to a brokerage related to one of the "big five" banks. The broker had to clear investments with me and I planned to keep equities under 50%. After five years the account had reached $750,000. Investments in equities averaged roughly 30% of the total portfolio. A summary of the transactions:

1. The broker bought 13 individual stocks with an average investment of $17,000. The 13 stocks were held for a weighted average of 550 days. In the 5 year period, 10 had been sold, 4 at a loss and 6 at a gain.
2. Of the 3 stocks still held at the end of the 5 year period 2 were down 21% and 88% and one was up 33%.
3. The average net capital gain was 13% on the 13 stocks picked by the broker (excluding any dividends received).
4. Roughly 4000 TSE equity index shares were purchased in the 5 years. None were sold and by the end of the five year measuring period the index had been owned for a weighted average of 750 days. Over the 5 year period the capital gain on the index shares was 49% (excluding any dividends received).
5. Interest income averaged over 5% per year.

If all of the stock investments by the broker would have been made in equity index funds the portfolio would have been worth $75,000 more at the end of the five year period. For this performance and particularly for buying Loewen (down 73%) and Laidlaw (down 88%), I moved the funds to another brokerage related to another of the "big five" banks. New cash of $190,000 and a portfolio with a market value of $750,000 from Broker 1 were handed to Broker 2 early in 2000.

Through December 31, 2007 here is what the broker accomplished:

1. Bought 13 different income trust units and all were sold by December 31, 1997. The average investment was $26,000 and the overall net capital gain was 6% over the period. This is only the gain/loss on share purchases and sales and does not include dividends received or additional tax benefits.
2. Bought 2 equity mutual funds for $70,000 in 2001 which were down in capital value by 16% and were still in the portfolio at December 31, 2007.
3. Bought and sold through the period 15 individual stocks with an average investment of $20,000 each. Twelve were sold generating capital gains and three were sold generating capital losses. The average capital net gain was 6%.

(continued)

CHAPTER SIX

(*continued*)

4. Inherited 4000 equity index shares from Broker 1 and within 18 months sold most of them, generating a net loss of roughly $10,000.
5. Bought at my request one individual stock we thought would have value. After holding it for three plus years it was sold for nickels. It is now trading for pennies.
6. Put into our portfolio an investment double the size of the normal investments we would make. The investment structure was far more complex than anything we had ever bought and should never have made it into our portfolio – but I did approve it in a brief telephone conversation. Immediately after issue it started to fade Less than a year later it was sold for a loss of $15,000. I believe I was victimized by the Monday morning Sales meeting and the need for the broker to sell $Y million of the notes the broker's firm was issuing for Corporation Z.

In the latter half of the measurement period monthly withdrawals were made, which caused some disruption undoubtedly. In total during the period when Broker #2 started net cash withdrawals totaled $450,000.

Over the whole period capital gains and capital losses netted to a trivial number. Dividend, interest and investment income was almost $400,000 and the portfolio ended at about $900,000. If none of the individual stocks, income trusts, and personal stock picks had been made and the investments in the original 4000 index shares had been held to December 31, 2007 the original investment of $150,000 would have grown to $325,000 a gain of $175,000. In this period the two Brokers together made investments of $1.25 million in individual stocks and realized a capital gain of $50,000.

Lessons I draw from this review:

1. Principles #2 and #3 are validated by my personal experience.
2. I have to be more forceful in directing the portfolio in the direction I want – eg. buying index shares. In spite of telling both brokers in advance that I was strongly in favour of equity funds, I believe neither of them ever recommended an investment in equity index funds.
3. I have to be more vigilant – do not allow the Monday morning sales meeting impact me again.

Soon I will retire and devote more time to my investments.

CONCLUSION

Well, that's Henry's story. A professional investor's experience during the past few decades of the ups and downs of the stock market. He concludes that active management of a portfolio usually doesn't even match the index – the return you would receive without any advice at all.

If you still believe the stock market is the way to secure your retirement, do you really think you can do better than Henry by using your current investment advisor?

PART TWO
THE DETAILS

Well there you have it – The Antidote – a six-point plan to guide you through the financial storm we are in. Remember, pick and choose what feels right for you. You don't have to follow all six points in order. You don't even have to follow all six of them. Follow even one and you'll probably improve your personal financial situation significantly.

Now let's go one step further – the details. In this section we'll explore the ins and outs of the CPP. We'll discover a simple way to answer the question about what age you should start to receive it. We'll also discover a tip that can save you thousands of dollars each and every year.

We'll also learn about the Money Maximizer spreadsheet and how to use this tool to maximize the money you and your family get to keep. I'll show you how you can get a free copy of it as a reader of this book.

We'll also address how the stock market is likely to behave in the future and the best ways to maximize your retirement income in this new economic reality we all face.

Lastly we'll look at alternatives to RRSPs. Can anything beat them? You'll know soon.

PART TWO

THE DETAILS

THE CANADA PENSION PLAN

WHAT IS THE CANADA PENSION PLAN?

The Canada Pension Plan (CPP) is a mandatory government-sponsored pension plan that came into effect on January 1, 1966 and was fully implemented on January 1, 1976. The only province that does not use the CPP is Quebec. They opted to create their own plan, the Quebec Pension Plan (QPP), which is similar to the CPP but supported by the provincial government.

The CPP is funded by Canadians that are employees, employers or self-employed. Contributions are required as soon as you reach the age of eighteen and are no longer required after you either reach the age of sixty-five or, become disabled.

Under the CPP, monthly pensions are paid to retirees, surviving spouses or common-law partners of deceased contributors, orphans, the disabled and children of the disabled. The term "common-law partners" came into force on July 30, 2000 and replaced the former term "spouse." This change broadened the entitlement to survivor's benefits to partners in same-sex relationships. A common-law partner is defined for CPP purposes as a person who is cohabiting with the contributor in a conjugal relationship at the relevant time, having so cohabited with the contributor for a continuous period of at least one year.

Lump-sum death benefits are also paid to the estate of deceased contributors. The amount is dependent on the contributions the deceased made to the CPP during his or her lifetime. The maximum lump-sum death benefit is currently $2,500.

It is important to note that the monthly benefits paid under the plan are adjusted annually, based on increases in the Consumer Price Index (CPI), the most common measure of inflation in Canada. In short, the CPP is an inflation-adjusted defined benefit pension plan that is paid until you die.

HOW THEY CALCULATE CPP PREMIUMS

Regular CPP premiums for employees are calculated at a rate of 4.95% of earnings above an exemption of $3,500 to a maximum of $52,500 in 2014. In other words, if you make under $3,500 you pay no CPP premiums and the maximum you pay is based on earnings up to $52,500 – if you earn more than that you only pay premiums on $52,500.

Here are the key figures for 2014:

Yearly Maximum Pensionable Earnings (YMPE)	$52,500
Yearly Basic Exemption	$3,500
Yearly Maximum Contributory Earnings	$49,000 ($52,500 less $3,500)
Yearly Maximum Contributions	$2,425.50 ($49,000.00 × 4.95%)

HOW THEY CALCULATE THE CPP PENSION

You may be wondering how they calculate the maximum monthly CPP retirement pension. It's pretty straightforward – it's 25% of the last five years' average maximum pensionable earnings (AMPE).

Table 7.1 shows how they got the maximum monthly CPP retirement pension for 2014.

HOW THE CPP ADJUSTS FOR INFLATION: THE YMPE

The YMPE is increased each year by the ratio of the average industrial aggregate (average weekly earnings), as determined by Statistics Canada, during the twelve-month period ending June 30 of

TABLE 7.1   Last five years Yearly Maximum Pensionable Earnings (YMPE)

2010	$47,200
2011	$48,300
2012	$50,100
2013	$51,100
2014	$52,500
Average of 2010 to 2014 YMPE (AMPE)	$49,840
25% of the AMPE	$12,460
Monthly ($12,460/12)	$1,038.33

the preceding year, to the average industrial aggregate during the corresponding period one year earlier.

The YMPE increased by 2.74% from 2013 to 2014 ($52,500 − $51,100 = $1,400, divided by $51,100 = 2.74%) because the average weekly earnings increased by that same percentage.

CPP PENSION

It is only after you begin to receive the CPP pension that the CPP plan uses the CPI to adjust your CPP pension amount. These increases are included so that contributions and benefits keep up with the cost of living.

Statistics Canada developed the CPI to measure changes in the cost of living. The main CPI index is called the All-items. It tracks the prices of a basket of approximately six hundred items, including typical household expenditures such as food, clothing, shelter, transportation and recreation, on a monthly basis.

They use 2002 as the base year for calculations. That is to say, the CPI index was made equal to 100 in June of 2002. This means that the defined basket of goods cost $100 in June 2002. The All-items CPI index was 125.9 in June 2014 meaning that same basket of goods would have cost $125.90 at that time.

The CPP pension is adjusted once a year using a twelve-month "moving average method," which helps to smooth out fluctuations that may occur in a single month. The rate used to increase the CPP pension is the average monthly All-items CPI index for the prior year's twelve-month period ending in October. They use October because they need to publish the rates for the next year in the fall of the previous year.

Here's how they got the rate to increase existing CPP pensions for 2014:

- average All-items CPI Index of all months November 2012 to October 2013 = 122.6
- average All-items CPI Index of all months November 2011 to October 2012 = 121.5

Percentage increase is 0.9% (122.6 − 121.5 = 1.1, divided into 121.5 = 0.9%).

Here's the good news: if the cost of living decreases over the twelve-month periods, the calculation of the rate increase would produce a negative amount but the CPP pension does not decrease in this case. It stays at the prior year's level.

Here's the bad news: Your CPP contribution rates increase every year by inflation, but since the retirement pension is calculated on the last five years' YMPE, it may lag current inflation.

THE NEW CPP RULES

Significant new rules regarding the CPP came into effect in 2011 that were approved in Bill C-51 that passed into law December 15, 2009.

Early election penalty

The normal age to elect your CPP retirement pension is sixty-five but you can elect to receive it as early as age sixty, but there is a cost to do so. Before the new rules came in, the penalty for early election was a reduction of 0.5% for each month that you elected to start receiving your pension before you turn sixty-five. That was 6% per year.

The new rules have increased this rate to 0.56% per month in 2014 (6.72% per year). It will be increasing to 0.58% per month in 2015 (6.96% per year) and 0.60% in 2016 (7.2% per year).

Deferring election premium

You can also elect to delay receiving the CPP pension until after age sixty-five to as late as age seventy. In this case you used to get a premium of 0.5% a month for each month you waited after you turned sixty-five. The new rules have increased this premium to 0.7% per month, or 8.4% per year.

Removal of work cessation test

Another change is the removal of the work cessation test for those under sixty-five that elect to receive the CPP early. Before 2012, for two months, the month before the CPP retirement pension was to begin and the month it did begin, you had to stop working or earn less than 25% of the CPP maximum pensionable earnings for the year of retirement and the preceding four years during those months.

Post-Retirement Benefit (PRB)

Under the old rules you could elect to start receiving your CPP before age sixty-five, then go back to work and you would no longer have to pay any more CPP premiums. The new rules have changed this. Now working beneficiaries under sixty-five are required to pay premiums to increase benefits. These premiums are the same as the regular premiums that everyone pays on their salary and self-employed earnings.

Like the CPP retirement pension, the amount of each PRB will depend on your level of earnings, the amount of CPP contributions you made during the previous year, and your age as of the effective date of the PRB.

The maximum PRB for one year is equal to one-fortieth of the maximum CPP retirement pension. If you contribute less than the maximum, the amount of the year's PRB will be proportional to your contributions. For example, if you contributed half of the maximum contribution level, you will receive 50 percent of the maximum PRB.

For each year that you make a valid contribution to the CPP while receiving your retirement pension, you become eligible for a PRB the following January.

If you pay any amounts into your PRB one year, the amount of CPP pension you receive the next year and every year thereafter, will increase (in addition to any inflationary increase). The PRB will increase your retirement income for each year of contributions.

Note that after age sixty-five up to age seventy, to opt out of continuing to pay CPP premiums, you need to file election form CPT30 – Election to stop contributing to the Canada Pension Plan, or revocation of a prior election.

There is an online calculator (http://www.servicecanada.gc.ca/eng/services/pensions/cpp/prb/index.shtml) that gives you an estimate of the yearly benefits you could receive from the PRB for a single year of contributions, based on your employment earnings for the year and your age. To see the table that is relevant to you, choose your year of birth from the pull-down menu.

DROP-OUT PROVISION

In calculating how much CPP you will receive, you are allowed to drop-out years of low earnings. The percentage of years allowed has increased from 15% (prior to 2012) to 17%. This means the number of years you can drop-out has gone from seven to eight years, since there are 47 years from age eighteen to sixty-five (47 × 15% = seven, 47 × 17% = eight).

Note that when these years were is irrelevant (i.e. early or later in life).

HOW TO APPLY FOR YOUR CPP PENSION

In order to start receiving the CPP pension, you must apply for it. Before you apply, you must:

- be at least a month past your fifty-ninth birthday;
- have contributed to the CPP; and
- want your retirement pension payments to begin within 11 months.

Although it is not a requirement, the government suggests you apply for your CPP pension six months before you want your pension to begin. Payment of the benefit also must be approved by the government.

You will need the following information:

- your Social Insurance Number (SIN);
- your banking information to arrange for direct deposit;
- your other ID number if you have worked or lived outside Canada and want to apply for benefits from that country; and
- your spouse or common-law partner's SIN should you want to take advantage of CPP pension sharing for possible tax savings.

You can either complete and submit the CPP retirement pension application online, or print the CPP retirement pension application form (ISP1000), complete it, and mail it to your nearest Service Canada office.

To apply online, go to http://www.servicecanada.gc.ca/eng/services/pensions/cpp/retirement/apply.shtml. Once you have filled out the form, you submit it electronically. Then you'll need to print and sign a signature page found in step seven of the application and mail it to Service Canada. A date stamp will appear on the signature page indicating the date and time the online portion of your application was sent. The date stamp is in Atlantic Standard Time (AST), and the time zone you are in and the day of the month you apply may affect the official receipt date of your application. You may also want to print a copy of step six "Confirm and Submit" for your own records.

If you need help you can call Service Canada at 1–800–277–9914 (English), 1–800–277–9915 (French) or 613–990–2244 (from all other countries, and they accept collect calls).

Applying to receive the CPP pension is an important step that some seniors are not aware of. There are many seniors that are not getting the money they deserve because they simply have not filled in the form. If you know any seniors, especially those newer to the country that may not speak either language very well, do them a favour and make sure they are receiving the CPP pension if they are eligible. It could make a significant difference to some of them.

You can also apply online using the "My Service Canada Account."

MY SERVICE CANADA ACCOUNT

The Federal government makes certain information, forms and services available online using a "My Service Canada Account."

It's accessible from the Service Canada website (http://www.servicecanada.gc.ca/eng/online/mysca.shtml) and it offers Service Canada online services through a single access point. This initiative is part of a plan to harmonize services and business processes between Service Canada and other government departments.

My Service Canada Account brings together CPP, Old Age Security (OAS) and Employment Insurance (EI) online services into a single portal. You can:

- apply for CPP Retirement pension
- view CPP Statement of Contributions online
- view and print tax information slips for CPP, OAS and EI
- apply for a personal access code for CPP and OAS
- access EI services;
- manage Records of Employment
- change your personal information (update your mailing address, telephone number, direct deposit information, etc.)

My Service Canada Account also includes links to other online services that are available outside the portal, such as the online CPP Retirement Application and the Canadian Retirement Income Calculator.

HOW TO REGISTER FOR MY SERVICE CANADA ACCOUNT

First, you will need an employment insurance access code or a personal access code (PAC). If you are an employment insurance claimant, use the access code found on your benefits statement. With this code you can use the register button on the My Service Canada web page mentioned above.

If you are not an employment insurance claimant, you'll need to request a PAC before registering. To obtain a PAC, you must provide your Social Insurance Number, first and last name, date of birth and your mother's last name at her birth. You must also provide your postal code if you are a Canadian resident or your country of residence if you are a foreign resident.

Once you have made your PAC request, CRA will mail it to you at the address they have on file for you. With your PAC you can then register for your My Service Canada Account on the same web page. Just click "register" on the same web page. Here you can register for your My Service Canada Account, which is called a "GCKey." To register for a GCKey, click "Continue to GCKey" and then click "Register." After accepting the terms and conditions, you can create your registration information. Here are the three steps:

1. **Create your user ID.** Your user ID must contain between eight and sixteen characters and may contain up to seven digits. It cannot contain special characters like %, # and @.
2. **Create your recovery questions.** These are used if you forget your password. They should be easy for you to remember but hard for others to guess. You can optionally use hints to assist you with remembering your answers. Your answers must contain at least three characters and no special characters. Your hints must contain at least three characters and may contain letters, numbers and the following punctuation characters: apostrophe ('), comma (,), dash (-), period (.) and question mark (?). You will need to create three questions: a recovery question (like what was the make of the first car you drove), a memorable person and a memorable date.
3. **Create your password.** It must be between eight and sixteen characters, contain at least one upper case letter, one lower case letter and one digit, and be different from your user ID.

At this stage you will be taken to the "GCKey registration complete" page. Click on "Continue" and you should be brought to the page to register for your My Service Canada Account. You will need to complete the following in order to register and validate your identity:

- your Social Insurance Number (SIN)
- your date of birth

- your EI access code or CPP/OAS personal access code
- your province or territory

After completing these steps, you will be presented with the My Service Canada Account home page.

On subsequent visits you will only need to provide your GCKey user ID and password to login to your My Service Canada Account.

Note that there is an option to sign-in using a "Sign-In Partner" which is your online banking information. At present there are only five Sign-In Partners: BMO Financial Group, Choice Rewards MasterCard, Scotiabank, Tangerine and TD Bank Group, but you will still need a PAC and a GCKey user ID and password.

HOW TO CALCULATE YOUR CPP RETIREMENT PENSION

The following section will take you step-by-step through the process to calculate how much you can expect from your CPP retirement pension. After all, that is all that matters, not what the maximum is or even the average.

I had been looking for this information for over ten years. The actual way the government does the calculation seems to be kept secret in some kind of "black box."

The story of how I got this is kind of interesting and illustrates the power of social media. I have a policy of accepting any invitations to connect on LinkedIn and one day I got a request from an individual named Doug Runchey. Here's what he said:

"David: Thanks for accepting my invitation to connect on LinkedIn. Please don't hesitate to contact me if you ever have any questions about CPP or OAS. I've only started my own business (http://www .drpensions.ca/index.html) recently, but I have over 30 years of prior experience working for the government on those two programs. Yours truly, Doug:)"

I had finally met someone who knows exactly how the CPP and OAS plans work.

Doug has written a detailed article titled "How to calculate your CPP retirement pension" and he has generously allowed me to use it here in this book. (The website www.retirehappy.ca has the full article with links to other related articles embedded in it.)

Here's how you calculate what CPP pension you will receive:

1. Register for a My Service Canada Account as described above and request the most recent copy of your CPP Statement of Contributions (SOC). Note that you can also request an estimate of your CPP benefits. This estimate is quite accurate if you are within a few years of starting to collect your CPP pension, but can be misleading if your future earnings will be significantly higher or lower than your previous average lifetime earnings.

2. Calculate your Number of Contributory Months (NCM). Note that the CPP plan deals in months, not years. Your contributory period begins either the month after you turn 18 or in January 1966, whichever is later (the CPP started in January 1966). It ends either the month you turn 70 or the month before the month that your CPP retirement pension starts, whichever is earlier. Your contributory period excludes any month that you received a CPP disability benefit.

   a. Your NCM would be the total number of months in your contributory period minus any months you received the CPP disability benefit. For example, the NCM for someone applying for the CPP at age sixty-five in 2014 or later, who had never received CPP disability benefits would be 564 months. That is 47 years from 18 to 65 times 12 months.

3. Calculate your Total Adjusted Pensionable Earnings (TAPE). Your CPP Statement of Contributions will give you a listing of your pensionable earnings for each year from age 18. These amounts are referred to as Unadjusted Pensionable Earnings (UPE). For each year, divide the UPE by the Year's Maximum Pensionable Earnings (YMPE). A listing of all YMPEs since the CPP began in 1966 can be found at www.drpensions.ca/cpp-rate-table.html. Then, for each year, multiply the result by the average YMPE for the five-year period ending in the year that your CPP will start.

a. For example, the average YMPE for the five-year period ending in 2014 is $49,840 as we have just seen. So if a person had a UPE of $4,000 in 1966 when the YMPE was $5,000, the calculation would be $4,000/$5,000 × $49,840 (the average YMPE for the five-year period ending in 2014). The resulting APE for 1966 would be $39,872. This essentially brings the earnings for each year up to the current year value. This means that if you were at the maximum in 1966 with a UPE of $5,000 when the YMPE was $5,000 it is worth the same as a UPE of $52,500 in 2014 (when the YMPE was $52,500) when calculating your CPP retirement pension.

b. Your Total Adjusted Pensionable Earnings (TAPE) is calculated by simply adding all the APE calculations for your entire contributory period.

4. Determine your Child Rearing Dropout Provision (CRDO). The first of the two main dropouts is the Child Rearing Provision (CRP). In this case dropouts are good because you are not penalized for having paid lower amounts into your CPP during those years. Under the CRP you can dropout any period of time that at least one child was under the age of 7 and where your APE was less than your average APE.

a. The period of CRDO eligibility starts with the month after the birth of the child and ends the month that child turns seven. If you have more than one child and they are born less than seven years apart, the period of eligibility starts the month following the birth of the oldest child and ends the month that the youngest child turns seven.

b. For example if you had three children born July 1980, May 1983 and June 1986, the period of CRDO eligibility would start August 1980 and end June 1993.

c. Note that the CRDO is not automatic, you must apply for it when you apply for your CPP pension. If you forgot to do that you can complete a separate form (ISP 1640) and submit it later as it is fully retroactive.

d. The CRDO is actually a two-step process. The first step (CRDO 1) allows a qualified parent to exclude any years from their contributory period where their earnings were less than the Year's Basic Exemption (generally $3,500). By excluding these years from their contributory period, CRDO 1 will increase the amount of their retirement pension and also help someone meet the eligibility criteria for disability and survivor benefits.

e. The second step (CRDO 2) allows a qualified parent to increase the amount of their CPP benefits by dropping out periods where their earnings were less than their average APE. To determine what years you can drop you need to calculate a temporary average monthly pensionable earnings (AMPE) value in order to see which months should be dropped out under CRDO 2. To do this, divide your total adjusted pensionable earnings (TAPE) by your number of contributory months (NCM, after excluding any periods of disability pension or CRDO 1 eligibility as mentioned above).

f. Any months of CRP eligibility where your adjusted pensionable earnings are less than this temporary AMPE value can now be dropped out under CRDO 1, along with the accompanying earnings.

Note that the CRP is done first and then the next dropout provision is applied.

5. Determine your General Dropout Provision. The general dropout, for which everyone is eligible, drops out a percentage of the lowest remaining earnings in your contributory period. The general dropout percentage from 2014 on is 17%. For example, for someone reaching age sixty-five in 2014, the contributory period would be 47 years or 564 months. If they never received CPP disability and weren't eligible for the CRP, they would remove the lowest 96 months of APE ($564 \times 17\%$ = 95.88, rounded up to 96 months or eight years).

a. If the same person was eligible for the CRP for two children born exactly three years apart, that person could drop out up to 10 of those years (or 120 months) under the CRP, plus a further 76 months under the general dropout provision ($(564-120) \times 17\%$ = 75.48, rounded up to 76).

b. Let's look at an example. Natalie worked full time for a couple of years after completing high school, and then had two children, born June 1979 and December 1982. She worked part-time until the second child turned seven, and then went back to work full-time and earned more than the Year's Maximum Pensionable Earnings every year until she turned 60, when she retired.

c. Without the Child Rearing Dropout Provision, Natalie's CPP retirement pension at age sixty-five would be significantly affected by her 10.5 years of part-time earnings that she had while raising her children because the general dropout provision would only allow her to drop only eight years – the five years of zero earnings after age 60 and three of the lowest years of part-time earnings. By dropping all of the 10.5 years under CRDO 2 and by using the general dropout to drop the five years of zero earnings after age 60, she can receive the maximum CPP retirement pension.

6. Calculate your Average Monthly Pensionable Earnings (AMPE). First, subtract all the APEs you identified in steps 4 and 5 as being dropped out from the TAPE you calculated in step 3. For example if you are dropping out 96 months, you would identify your eight years of lowest earnings and subtract the APEs for those years from the TAPE. The result is the TAPE (after dropout).

a. If you are dropping out less than a full year of APE, just pro-rate the amount. For example, if you are dropping out 76 months, you would drop out your lowest six full years of APE, and four months of the next lowest year. When dropping out the four months, you would drop 4/12ths of that calculated APE for that year.

b. Next, subtract the number of months identified as dropout periods in steps 4 and 5 from your original number of contributory months (NCM) calculated in step 2, to get your NCM (after dropout).

c. For example, if you only had the general dropout provision, 564 NCM less 96 months dropped out = 468 NCM (after dropout).

d. Your AMPE is simply your TAPE (after dropout) divided by your NCM (after dropout).

7. Calculate your Retirement for Benefit Calculation (RTR-FBC). This is simply 25% of your AMPE that is calculated in step 6. It is the amount your monthly CPP retirement pension will be if your pension is starting the month after you turn sixty-five.

8. If you elect to start before age sixty-five. If you are starting your CPP before age sixty-five, you'll need to decrease your RTR-FBC calculated in step 7 by the appropriate age factor. In 2014 this factor is 0.56% per month, for 2015 it's 0.58% per month and starting in 2016 it's 0.60% per month. In other words, you get this much less for each month you apply early.

   That means that for a person who applies for and receives their CPP retirement pension at age 60 they would have a reduction of 33.6% if taken in 2014, 34.8% if taken in 2015 and 36% if taken in 2016.

9. If you elect to start after age sixty-five. If you wait until after age sixty-five to start your CPP pension, you will get an increase of your RTR-FBC calculated in step 7 of 0.7% per month (8.4% per year).

   a. If you delay, there is also an additional dropout provision called the after-sixty-five dropout. Under this provision one of two things will happen:
   - If you are still working after age sixty-five, you can use these earnings to replace any periods of time under age sixty-five where you had lower APE;
   - If you are not working after age sixty-five or if your earnings after age sixty-five are less than any of your under-age sixty-five APE, you can simply dropout all periods after age sixty-five from both your NCM and your APE.

If you find the process too confusing or complex, you can email Doug at DRpensions@shaw.ca along with your CPP Statement of Contributions and any scenarios for which you want CPP retirement pension calculations done and he will do them for you for a small fee

(Disclosure: I do not receive any compensation for referring people – I do it because it is a very valuable service that is difficult to find).

MONEY SAVING TIP – CPP PENSION SHARING

As we have discussed, the most important method of saving taxes in Canada is to optimize the split of income on the tax returns belonging to you, your spouse or common-law partner and your children. This also applies to the Canada Pension Plan.

Under the CPP, common-law partners or spouses in an ongoing relationship, who are both at least sixty years old and who receive CPP retirement pension payments, can apply to share their CPP retirement pension payments by assigning a portion of the contributor's retirement income to his or her common-law partner or spouse.

Essentially, the government allows you to decide how much of one contributor's CPP pension can be shown on the other spouse's personal income tax return. The tax savings of this can be large, especially if one spouse has been the only breadwinner throughout the relationship.

You or your spouse or common-law partner can apply to receive an equal share of the retirement pensions you both earned during the years you were together. The amounts depend on how long you lived together and your contributions to the CPP during that time.

CPP PENSION SHARING EXAMPLE

Pension sharing adjusts the amount of the monthly CPP retirement pension each spouse or common-law partner receives from the CPP.

For example, if you lived together for twenty-five years during both your contributory periods:

Here's how it would work:

Kyle and Emma have been living together in a common-law relationship since 1979. They are both over sixty years old and both receive a CPP retirement pension.

Emma's monthly retirement pension is $400. Of that, $100 is based on income earned before moving in with Kyle; this *amount will not be affected by a pension-sharing arrangement. The other $300 is based on income earned during their relationship.*

Kyle was not working before this relationship. Kyle's monthly retirement pension of $550 is based entirely on income earned while living with Emma.

Their pension payments, added together, total $950. After subtracting the portion of Emma's pension that is based on income earned before moving in with Kyle ($100), their "shareable" pension amount is $850. With pension sharing, they would each receive half of $850, or $425. In addition to the $425, Emma would also receive the $100 that is based on earnings prior to this relationship with Kyle. Emma's total monthly CPP payment would be $525, while Kyle's would be $425.

Their T4A(P) – Statement of Canada Pension Plan Benefits slips will show the amount each received during the previous year and will be used when calculating their income tax.

Your pension sharing arrangement stops in whichever of the following month occurs first:

- the month after the month Service Canada approves a cancellation request submitted by both you and your spouse or common-law partner (this is Cancellation of Pension Sharing form ISP1014 available at http://www.servicecanada.gc.ca/eforms/forms/sc-isp-1014(2011-11-15)e.pdf;
- the month you divorce;
- the month the spouse or common-law partner who has never paid into the CPP (or QPP) begins contributing;
- the month one of you dies (you need to contact Service Canada as soon as possible to notify them of the date of death of the CPP pensioner/beneficiary).

Pension sharing only starts when your application is approved and the government does not allow you to backdate the sharing arrangement, so if it is of benefit to you, do not hesitate to apply. Either you or your spouse or common-law partner can apply.

The application form is pension sharing form ISP1002 and is available on the web at http://www.servicecanada.gc.ca/eforms/forms/ sc-isp-1002(2012–09–10)e.pdf.

Note that the overall benefits paid do not increase or decrease with pension sharing and that the new Post-Retirement Benefit is not eligible for CPP pension sharing.

WHEN SHOULD I ELECT TO RECEIVE CPP?

Unfortunately, just like with many decisions related to personal finance, there is no easy answer. Rules of thumb simply do not work. The main reason for this is that you need to know one important thing: when are you going to live until? Now that's a tough one to answer isn't it? Yes it is but it makes a huge difference to the calculations.

For example, say you retired at age sixty and end up passing away at age sixty-seven. If you elected early, at age sixty, you would have received your CPP retirement pension at a reduced rate for seven years. If you had waited until age sixty-five you would have only received the full pension for two years. If you crunch the numbers you'd see that you would have been better off electing at age sixty since the greater number of years you collected the reduced pension outweighs the lesser number of years for the full one. Put simply, the reduction penalty of 30% to 36% of the amount at age sixty-five (five years early × 6% under the old rules and 7.2% under the rules in 2016) is not overcome by waiting because you only get the higher rate for two years in this case.

On the other hand if you actually live to the ripe old age of 95, you'd see that it would be best to wait until age sixty-five to receive your CPP pension because you would be receiving the full amount for thirty years.

So where does that leave us? Since it is impossible to do a detailed calculation because we don't know how long we will be receiving the CPP pension, the best option is to go through a simple checklist that includes the important issue of taxes because the CPP pension is taxable when you receive it. Here is the thought process I recommend you go through:

Step 1

Do you need the money early? If the answer is yes, you need the money for groceries and other expenses, elect as soon as you can. End of story.

Step 2

If you don't really need the money, are you in a low tax bracket? If you are, consider electing early if you could use the money and you may be in a higher tax bracket later.

Step 3

When received will your CPP pension be taxed (possibly at a high rate) or could you shelter it from tax by making an RRSP contribution for the same amount? If you are in a high bracket and have maxed out your RRSP room, defer electing until later since you will lose up to half of your early CPP pension to taxes.

Step 4

If the answer to step 3 was that you had RRSP room to shelter your CPP, do you think the amount in your RRSP will grow at a higher rate than the penalties to elect early or the bonus to wait? Remember those rates for early election were 6.72% in 2014, 6.96% in 2015 and 7.2% in 2016. Those rates will be extremely difficult to beat after investment fees on a consistent basis.

In a nutshell, it seems that the government has achieved its objective of making early election less attractive to the majority of Canadians. It seems waiting is the best thing to do unless it is likely you will not live a nice long life.

WARNINGS

When it comes to the CPP there is something important that seniors need to be aware of – the impact of one spouse dying.

When one spouse dies it can have a significant effect on the total CPP pension amount that will be received by the surviving spouse.

When a CPP contributor dies, CPP pays three kinds of Survivor Benefits:

1. **The death benefit.** This is a one-time lump-sum payment (currently a maximum of $2,500);
2. **The childrens' benefit.** This monthly amount is paid to a dependent natural or adopted child of the deceased contributor, or a child in the care and control of the deceased contributor at the time of death. The child must be either under age eighteen, or between the ages of eighteen and twenty-five and in full-time attendance at a school or university.
3. **The survivor's benefit.** This is a monthly benefit for the spouse or common-law partner.

To qualify for any or all of these benefits, the deceased contributor must have contributed to the CPP for a minimum of three years.

If you are receiving your CPP retirement pension and your spouse or common-law partner dies, you need to apply for a survivor's benefit. In this case you will receive a combined monthly benefit.

Catch #1

The amount of a combined survivors/retirement benefit is limited to the maximum retirement pension. For example, if you begin receiving a combined benefit in 2014, the most you will receive is $1,038.33 a month. In other words, if you have been eligible to receive the maximum CPP pension because you contributed to the plan during your working life, you won't receive anything extra on the death of your spouse or common-law partner.

Catch #2

If the surviving spouse or common-law partner is age sixty-five or older and not receiving any CPP benefits of their own, they are eligible for a maximum of only 60% of the contributor's retirement pension. It should be noted that the rules in this area are exceedingly complex for people under sixty-five, people with disabilities and situations involving dependent children.

Catch #3

There's also the shock of the surviving spouse losing the deceased spouse's OAS pension – a maximum of $6,677 per year in 2014.

For couples on a tight budget these issues can lead to significant financial difficulties for the surviving spouse or common-law partner.

CONCLUSION

OK. There you have it. All you need to know about the CPP plan and how to calculate and optimize the amount you get out of it. Has your financial advisor discussed all this with you? He or she should have – it's a key part of your retirement strategy.

THE MONEY MAXIMIZER

Let's face it, we'd all like more money right? Well what's the best way to get it?

We could try to find another job that pays more. Perhaps we could work a lot more hours in our existing job in the hopes of getting a raise. If we are self-employed we could put in more hours at work in the hopes of making more profit.

Alternatively we could cut down our expenses by maybe forgoing a vacation this year or reducing our entertainment budget. Either way – increasing our income or reducing our expenses – it's likely to be a somewhat painful experience.

Would you be willing to spend a few hours looking at your financial big picture to see if there is something about your financial life that you could change to increase your cash flow? What if there was a spreadsheet that would allow you to calculate the total cash inflow in your entire life under many different scenarios so that you could choose the one that maximizes your family's cash inflows – without the pain of working more hours or reducing the expenses that make your life more enjoyable?

Well there is such a spreadsheet. It's called the "Money Maximizer" and I'm going to show it to you in this chapter.

WHY WORK AGAINST THE TAXMAN?

When we talk about maximizing your money, we are actually talking about maximizing your after-tax cash inflows. For example, we have seen that if you make $80,000 in salary in 2014 in Ontario, you would owe $18,087.85 in federal and Ontario income taxes, $2,425.50 in CPP and $913.67 in EI premiums. Total deductions would therefore be $21,427.02 ($18,087.85 + $2,425.50 + $913.67), leaving you with only $58,572.98 in after-tax cash ($80,000 − $21,427.02). You make $80,000 but you can't spend all of it because you have to pay tax and other deductions first.

If there was a way to reduce your taxes by perhaps $3,000, you would be left with $61,572.98 in after-tax cash – an additional $3,000 that you can do with as you please. That's a lot easier than working harder to earn additional salary, since that additional salary is taxed. That's like trying to run a race carrying a fifty-pound sack of potatoes – the additional taxes weigh you down.

For example, in Ontario in 2014 you would have to increase your salary by $4,634, to $84,634, to be left with $61,572.98, the amount you were left with by reducing your taxes by $3,000. That's because in that tax bracket, an additional $4,634 in salary attracts $1,634 in federal and Ontario income taxes, leaving you with an additional $3,000 in after-tax cash.

THE VALUE OF TIME

There is another concept that is key to maximizing your after-tax income: the time value of money. It's so important I'd like to review it again before we start.

Put simply, a dollar saved today is worth more than a dollar saved a year from now. That just makes sense. If you had a dollar today you could spend it, or invest it, or pay down debt with it. If you had to wait a year for that dollar, it would be worth less because you had to forego the spending, couldn't invest it to earn a rate of return and couldn't pay down debt with it to reduce your interest expenses.

But how much less is that dollar worth? Well, it depends in something called the "discount rate." That's the interest rate that's in effect for the situation. For example, if you could invest that dollar in a GIC earning 5% a year, the discount rate to use is 5%. Using a discount rate of 5% on a dollar received a year from now yields a net present value (NPV) of $0.95 (actually $0.9523). In other words,

$0.95 invested today would be worth $1 a year from now because $0.95 times 1.05 is $1.

Don't worry if you don't really grasp the concept of discount rates and NPV calculations – you don't really need to. But you need to buy into the concept because it is absolutely vital when you start talking about large dollar values over many years. Let's look at that now.

THE TIME VALUE OF MONEY

When we talk about retirement planning, the long term is basically your lifetime. For you it doesn't get any longer than that.

Say you are thirty years old and live to age ninety. That's sixty years of time you have to deal with. But what you do at age thirty is incredibly more significant than what you do at age sixty. In other words, if you can save $1,000 at age thirty, the benefit to you is much greater than if you saved $1,000 at age sixty.

That's why in the following discussions, I will always mention the NPV affect of any change. It will effectively show the significance of a change in strategy, taking into account when it happens – the time value of money. For example, in the previous case, a change in strategy that saves us $1,000 this year is worth $1,000 in NPV. Saving $1,000 thirty years from now is only worth $231 today discounted at 5% a year.

THE MONEY MAXIMIZER SPREADSHEET

The Money Maximizer is a spreadsheet that will show you the after-tax cash inflow of you and your spouse or common-law partner from today to the end of your projected lifespans, taking into account federal and provincial income taxes for Alberta, British Columbia, Manitoba, Nova Scotia, Ontario, and Saskatchewan. It will show you the total after-tax cash inflows from today until the end of both your lives, as well as the NPV of those future cash flows.

As we saw in the chapter on income splitting, the key to reducing your family's income taxes is to focus on your as well as your spouse's or common-law partner's tax situation. That's why the spreadsheet has a column for you and your spouse or common-law partner – side-by-side – so that you can see the effect on your bottom line, your combined after-tax cash flows.

The real value of the spreadsheet is that it allows you to change variables such as amounts, rates of return and time frames to see what the effect is on your after-tax cash inflows – the total as well as the NPV of your and your spouse's total cash inflows during your lifetimes.

It has the following worksheets or tabs shown at the bottom of the screen that you can click on to go to a separate section of the same spreadsheet:

- **Home**. Tells you a bit about the spreadsheet, including the version number and what it does.
- **Questions**. This is where you and your spouse or common-law partner answer all the questions needed to do the calculations.
- **Summary 30–95**. This is the summary screen showing all the information about each of you and your spouse's or common-law partner's income, taxes and after-tax cash inflows for as many as sixty-five years. It also shows the combined after-tax cash flows discounted to the present day – the NPV of all future after-tax cash flows. You should pick the tab that applies for your province, Alberta (AB), British Columbia (BC), Manitoba (MB), Nova Scotia (NS), Ontario (ON) and Saskatchewan (SK).
- **Retirement Results You.** This tab shows the year-by-year income from your RRSP, OAS, CPP and RRIF withdrawals (minimum and additional to meet your cash flow needs) from as early as age fifty-five to age ninety-five. It also tracks your RRSP and RRIF values to show whether you'll run out of money while you still have need for it.
- **Retirement Results Spouse.** The same as the previous tab, but for your spouse or common-law partner.
- **Assumptions.** These are the assumptions that went into the spreadsheet.
- **Taxinfo.** This tab has all the tax, CPP, OAS rates and amounts as well as the minimum RRIF withdrawal percentages.
- **Release notes.** This tab shows the changes made for each version of the spreadsheet.

The following is a screen shot of the Home screen of the Money Maximizer:

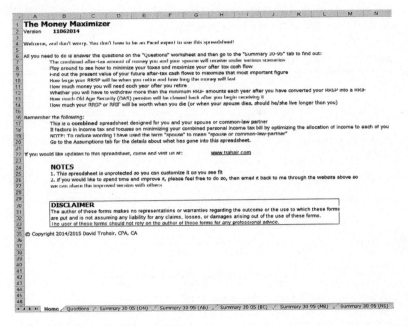

Note the tabs at the bottom. The Home tab is the active tab and is shown in bold.

MEET PAT AND JANE

In this chapter and throughout the remainder of this book I will be using an example of a married Canadian couple named Pat and Jane. In this case Pat is "You" and Jane is the "Spouse" (I have used "spouse" to mean "spouse or common-law partner" to save space in the spreadsheet). These individuals are fictitious and their situation will almost certainly not be the same as yours but here's the good part: the spreadsheet is available to you free as a reader of this book. Simply go to http://www.trahair.com and click on "David's Books" on the list on the left side of the page, then click the link to the cover of this book. The Excel spreadsheet then can be downloaded to your computer for your own use.

Here are all the answers Pat and Jane punched into the "Questions" tab on the spreadsheet. Please bookmark this page, as we will be investigating the financial affect of making changes to one or more of the answers that Pat and Jane have given here:

TABLE 8.1 Pat and Jane's Answers: General

GENERAL		
	Pat	**Jane**
What is today's date?	11–06–2014	11–06–2014
What is your last name?	Smith	Smith
What is your first name?	Pat	Jane
On what day were you born?	15–11–1978	15–06–1983
In what province/territory do you reside?	Ontario	Ontario
Would you like to split your pension income with your spouse?	N	N
Would you like to split your CPP pension income with your spouse?	N	N
What discount rate would you like to use to calculate the Net Present Value (NPV) of future cash flows?	5.00%	5.00%

TABLE 8.2 Pat and Jane's Answers: Income/Expenses

INCOME/EXPENSES		
What is your current gross salary (before tax)?	$90,000	$0
What is your current net income from self-employment?	$0	$0
What percent of your self-employment earnings (if any) could you split with your spouse?	0.00%	0.00%
How much money (before tax) from other sources in today's dollars do you expect each year after you retire? (For example, pension, self-employment, rental, investments outside RRSP)	$0	$0
At what age do you expect this income from other sources to stop?	80	85
What percentage of your income before tax in today's dollars do you think you will need after you retire? (Note: The rule of thumb says about 70%, but depending on your situation it could be much lower – perhaps 40%)	50.00%	50.00%

TABLE 8.3   Pat and Jane's Answers: RRSP/RRIF

RRSP/RRIF		
What was the total market value of your RRSPs on the most recent statement?	$55,000	$0
How much do you plan to contribute to your RRSP each year from now until retirement?	$8,000	$0
At what age do you plan to retire and stop making RRSP contributions?	65	65
At what annual rate of return do you expect your RRSP investments to grow **until** you retire?	5.00%	5.00%
At what annual rate of return do you expect your RRSP or RRIF investments to grow **after** you retire?	4.00%	4.00%
What average annual rate of inflation do you expect over the remainder of your life?	2.00%	2.00%

TABLE 8.4   Pat and Jane's Answers: Old Age Security

OLD AGE SECURITY		
Are you eligible for the maximum Old Age Security (OAS) pension? (Y = Yes, N = No) (If you have lived in Canada for at least 40 years after turning 18, you will receive the maximum pension)	Y	Y
If not, how many years will you have lived in Canada since your 18th birthday when you turn 65? (You must have lived in Canada for at least 10 years to qualify for OAS)		

TABLE 8.5   Pat and Jane's Answers: Canada Pension Plan

CANADA PENSION PLAN		
Are you eligible for the maximum Canada Pension Plan (CPP) pension at age 65? (Y = Yes, N = No) (If on average from age 18 to retirement your earnings exceeded the maximum pensionable earnings ($52,500 in 2014), you should receive the maximum CPP pension)	Y	N
If not, what has your average annual income from earnings been since you turned 18? (Enter a figure between $0 and $52,500)	$0	$0
Would you like to start receiving your CPP pension between the ages of 60 and 65? (It will be reduced by a percentage for each year before age 65 – see question below)	N	N
If so, at what age would you like to start receiving your CPP pension? (Enter an age between 60 and 64)	62	62
If you elect to receive your CPP early, what annual penalty rate would you like to use? (2014 = 6.72%, 2015 = 6.96%, 2016 = 7.2%)	6.72%	6.72%

TABLE 8.6   Pat and Jane's Answers: Longevity

LONGEVITY		
Until what age do you think you will live? (Must be age 70 or older)	82	82

Here's a screen shot of the top section of the "Questions" tab of the spreadsheet:

FIGURE 8.1   Money Maximizer Questions

A WORD ABOUT DATE FORMATS (MM/DD/YEAR VS DD/MM/YEAR)

It always used to confuse me when typing dates as numbers – is it MM/DD/YEAR or DD/MM/YEAR. It's not confusing for days after the twelfth of the month, but for days one to twelve it is.

For example is 1/6/2014 January 6, 2014 (MM/DD/YEAR) or June 1, 2014 (DD/MM/YEAR)? The answer seems to be that in Canada the accepted format is DD/MM/YEAR and in the U.S. it's MM/DD/YEAR. That confuses me because I find the MM/DD/YR format easier to understand. I am interested in knowing the month before the day since it's more important. It's also the order I would write it if I was using the words for the month, i.e., I would write "January 6, 2014" not "6 January, 2014".

That used to leave me as a Canadian using the accepted U.S. format. But over the years this has led to some confusion when using Excel. As a result I have switched to the accepted Canadian format of DD/MM/YEAR. This is easy to set on your computer so that your dates show up in a consistent way in the various programs you use (such as Microsoft Excel). To set it up in Microsoft Windows go to the "Start" button then select "Control Panel" then "Regional and Language Options." Here if you select "English (Canada)" it will show the "Short date" format as DD/MM/YEAR.

PAT AND JANE: THE ASSUMPTIONS

The beauty of a spreadsheet is that you can change any variable you wish to see what the effect is on after-tax cash flow is. In this case I have made the following assumptions. Remember, you can make your own assumptions for your own situation:

- **Salary**. I have added an inflation factor to Pat's $90,000 salary by increasing it at the rate of inflation input above of 2% a year from this year (age thirty-five) until age sixty-five.
- **RRSP Contributions**. I have kept Pat's RRSP contributions constant at $8,000 a year.
- **OAS and CPP pension income**. I have increased these amounts by the 2% inflation rate, as this is what the government does.
- **Income Tax Rates**. Income taxes are computed for all years at 2013 rates.
- **RRSP and RRIF withdrawals**. These are assumed to take place on January 1 of each year.
- **Basic personal exemption and age amounts**. Have not been indexed to inflation.

A NOTE ABOUT PROJECTIONS

A projection like the one the Money Maximizer produces will never give an exact answer because the future has many unknowns. For example, tax rates and personal exemptions will most certainly change. RRSP limits and minimum RRIF withdrawals might change. There is also uncertainty about income – very few people will have full-time employment each and every year with a salary that rises by inflation.

The key point, however, is that the Money Maximizer does provide an excellent way to compare one situation to another. For example, say we want to compare earning a salary to earning a similar amount of self-employment income, allowing us to split income with our spouse. We assume the basic personal exemption stays at $11,138 for the next sixty years, which most certainly won't be the case. Because the basic personal exemption will change in future years, the spreadsheet won't give us a perfect figure for the after-tax cash inflows. But it will provide an accurate calculation of the *difference* between the two situations, and that's key to our decision making. Let's move on and you'll see what I mean.

PAT AND JANE: THE RESULTS

The Money Maximizer projects that if Pat and Jan lived in Ontario, their after-tax cash inflows from 2014 to 2066, the year of Jane's death, will total $3,953,939. That is a lot of dough.

But what about on a discounted basis, the more important figure because it takes into account the time value of money?

That total is $1,449,155, still a significant sum, but much less than $3.954 million. That's because in this case, as in your case, a lot of the cash flow is received many years from now and must be discounted to today's dollars so we can compare apples to apples.

Here's a screen shot of the top section of the "Summary 30–95 (ON)" tab of the spreadsheet:

FIGURE 8.2   Money Maximizer Summary

	A	B	C	D	F	G	H	I
1	Money Maximizer Summary Results ONTARIO							
2								
3								
4				Tax	Pat	Jane	Pat	Jane
5				Form	35	30	36	31
6				Line	2014	2014	2015	2015
7	Total income							
8	Employment income (box 14 T4 slip)		101	Auto	90,000	0	91,800	0
9	Old Age Security pension (box 18 T4A(OAS) slip)		113	Auto	0	0	0	0
10	CPP or QPP benefits (box 20 T4A(P) slip) (Age 60 and older)		114	Auto	0	0	0	0
11	CPP pension split (You to Spouse)			Auto	0	0	0	0
12	CPP pension split (Spouse to You)			Auto	0	0	0	0
13	Other pensions or superannuation			Auto	0	0	0	0
14	Elected split-pension amount (Form T1032)		115	ENTER	0	0	0	0
15	RRIF minimum withdrawals (Age 72 and older)		116	Auto	0	0	0	0
16	RRIF extra withdrawals (Age 72 and older if needed)			Auto	0	0	0	0
17	RRIF value taxed on death			ENTER	0	0	0	0
18	Taxable amount of eligible dividends			Blank				
19	Actual dividend x 1.45 (Public Companies)		120	ENTER				
20	Taxable amount of ineligible dividends			Blank				
21	Actual dividend x 1.25 (Small Businesses)		180	ENTER				
22	Interest and other investment income (Schedule 4)		121	ENTER				
23	Rental income (net)		126	ENTER				
24	Taxable capital gains (50% of actual net gains Schedule 3)		127	ENTER				
25	RRSP income (T4RSP slips) (Age 55 to 71)							
26	Other income (CPP ineligible) (Age 55 and older)		129	Auto	0	0	0	0
27	Self-employment income (net)		130	Auto	0	0	0	0
28	Self-employment transfer (You to Spouse)		135	Auto	0	0	0	0
29	Self-employment transfer (Spouse to You)			Auto	0	0	0	0
30	This is your total income		150	Auto	90,000	0	91,800	0
31								
32	Net income							
33	Registered pension plan deduction (box 20 T4, box 32 T4A)		207	ENTER				
34	RRSP deduction (Schedule 7)		208	Auto	8,000	0	8,000	0
35	Deduction for elected split-pension amount (Form T1032)		210	Auto	0	0	0	0
36	Child care expenses (Form 778)		214	ENTER				
37	Carrying charges and interest expenses (Schedule 4)		221	ENTER				
38	Deduction for CPP contributions on self-employment		222	Auto	0	0	0	0
39	Total line 207 to 222		233		8,000	0	8,000	0
40	This is your net income before adjustments		234		82,000	0	83,800	0
41	Social benefits repayment (OAS Clawback)		235	Auto	0	0	0	0
42	This is your net income		236	Auto	82,000	0	83,800	0
43								
44	Taxable income							
45	Net capital losses of other years		253	ENTER				
46	Capital gains deduction		254	ENTER				
47								
48	Total Further deductions			Auto	0	0	0	0
49								
50	This is your taxable income		260	Auto	82,000	0	83,800	0
51								

Home / Questions / Summary 30–95 (ON) / Summary 30–95 (AB) / Summary 30–95 (BC) / Summary 30–95 (MB) / Summa

And here is a screen shot of the same tab but further down, showing the total after-tax cash inflows on a non-discounted and discounted basis:

FIGURE 8.3 Money Maximizer Summary Showing Total After-tax Cash Inflows on a Non-discounted and Discounted Basis

	A	B	C	D	F	G	H	I
1	Money Maximizer Summary Results ONTARIO							
2								
3				Tax	Pat	Jane	Pat	Jane
4				Form	35	30	36	31
5				Line	2014	2014	2015	2015
6								
7	Total income							
38	Deduction for CPP contributions on self-employment	222		Auto	0	0	0	0
39	Total line 207 to 222	233			8,900	0	8,000	0
40	This is your net income before adjustments	234			82,900	0	83,800	0
41	Social benefits repayment (OAS Clawback)	235		Auto	0	0	0	0
42	This is your net income	236		Auto	82,900	0	83,800	0
43								
44	Taxable income							
45	Net capital losses of other years	253	ENTER					
46	Capital gains deduction	254	ENTER					
47								
48	Total Further deductions			Auto	0	0	0	0
49								
50	This is your taxable income	260		Auto	82,900	0	83,800	0
51								
52	Refund or Balance owing							
53	Net federal tax (Schedule 1 line 52)	420		Auto	11,025	0	11,421	0
54	CPP contributions payable of self-employment earnings (Schedule 8)	421		Auto	0	0	0	0
55	Social benefits repayment (OAS clawback line 235)	422		Auto	0	0	0	0
56	Provincial or territorial tax (Form 428)	428		Auto	5,734	0	5,975	0
57	This is your total payable	435			16,758	0	17,395	0
58								
59								
60	After-tax Cash Inflow Before CPP and EI			Auto	65,242	0	66,405	0
61	(Equals Net Income less Total Payable)							
62								
63	TOTAL AFTER-TAX CASH INFLOW							
64	After-tax Cash Inflow Before CPP and EI				65,242	0	66,405	0
65	Add: Self-employment CPP deduction				0	0	0	0
66	Less:							
67	CPP contributions through employment				-2,356	0	-2,356	0
68	Employment insurance premiums				-891	0	-891	0
69								
70	TOTAL AFTER-TAX CASH INFLOW				61,995	0	63,158	0
71								
72								
73	Combined Annual After-tax Cash Inflow			Auto	61,995		63,158	
74								
75	Total Combined After-tax Cash Inflows				3,953,939			
76								
77	Net Present Value all Future After-tax Cash Inflows at 5% per year			Auto	1,449,155			
78								
79	CALCULATION AREA BELOW THIS LINE							
80								

Home / Questions / Summary 30-95 (ON) / Summary 30-95 (AB) / Summary 30-95 (BC) / Summary 30-95 (MB) / Summar

PAT AND JANE TRY INCOME SPLITTING

Currently Pat earns a salary of $90,000 a year and Jane does not work. This puts Pat in a high tax bracket and does not take advantage of Jane being in the lowest bracket.

What do you think the dollar affect would be if Pat could split, or allocate, some of the income to Jane? Unfortunately, if Pat has a normal salaried job, the ability to split income is limited. If Pat was a self-employed person, things could change.

Let's say Pat earns self-employment earnings of $90,000 instead of salary, and then could pay a wage to Jane for services such as book-keeping, sales and marketing, or strategic planning for Pat's business. We'll assume a wage of $27,000 (30% of $90,000) is reasonable.

We'll also assume Pat's $90,000 self-employment income increases at the 2% inflation rate, as we did previously when it was salary.

All we need to do is change a couple of answers on the "Questions" tab in the spreadsheet. We change the answer to the question "What is your current gross salary (before tax)?" to zero, and enter $90,000 in response to the question "What is your current net income from self-employment?" We also change the answer to "What percent of your self-employment earnings (if any) could you split with your spouse?" to 30%.

You may also note another interesting affect: Jane now has earnings and must contribute to the CPP. She will therefore be building up her CPP retirement nest egg and will be able to rely on that income from as early as age sixty.

We'll need to change Jane's answer to the question under the CPP heading because she is under the maximum pensionable earnings for CPP of $52,500 (for 2014). We input $27,000 – the amount of income allocated from Pat for 2014.

If we move to the "Summary 30–95 (ON)" tab we'll see that in 2014 Pat's $90,000 in self-employment income now shows on the self-employment income line rather than the employment income line in the column for Pat in 2014 (age thirty-five).

The results? Total combined after-tax cash inflows are $4,293,389 – $339,450 more than if Pat were salaried ($4,293,389 – 3,953,939). The NPV of the future after-tax cash flows is $1,518,980 – ahead of the salaried scenario by $69,825 ($1,518,980 – $1,449,155).

The conclusion is not that Pat should simply become self-employed. That may be impossible given the circumstances. Maybe in Pat's line of work you need to be salaried, or maybe Pat can't stand the idea of being self-employed. That's not the point. The point is that the spreadsheet empowers you to play with "what-if" scenarios to see what effect a decision might have on the big picture – your family's combined after-tax cash inflows.

PUTTING THE RRSP "START LATE" THEORY TO THE TEST

But let's put the "start late" theory to the test with Pat and Jane. Pat has $55,000 in an RRSP and contributes $8,000 per year for thirty-one years (from age thirty-five to age sixty-five). And we have assumed the RRSP grows by 5% per year.

At age sixty-five Pat's RRSP had built up to a value of $769,218 and provided sufficient income to Pat's expiration at age eighty-two.

Let's assume Pat and Jane buy a house in 2019, when Pat is forty years old, for $333,333. They put a down payment of $83,333 from an inheritance and assume a mortgage of $250,000 for the remainder.

You can easily do a Google search of the web for "Mortgage Calculator" to find websites that will calculate mortgage payments. I just punched in a $250,000 mortgage amount, at 6% a year over an amortization period of twenty-five years. The online calculator yielded a monthly payment of $1,599.52. That is $19,194.24 annually. Assuming the interest rate stays the same for the twenty-five years, this mortgage would be paid off in 2044 when Pat was sixty-five years old.

Let's look at doing things differently. Pat and Jane decide at Pat's age of thirty-five that they don't want to follow the "RRSP at all costs" route to retirement savings. They decide to forego any RRSP contributions until the mortgage is paid off. Will they be able to build up an RRSP of $769,218 by Pat's sixty-fifth birthday? Let's see.

From now (2014) until 2019 when they buy the house, Pat does not make the $8,000 annual RRSP contribution. This is where the Money Maximizer spreadsheet comes in handy. I simply changed Pat's RRSP contribution answer to $0 from $8,000. The tax bill for Pat in 2014 went to $19,803 from $16,758 – an increase of $3,045. That means Pat has a marginal tax rate of 38.1%, including Ontario surtaxes. So Pat is left with an extra $4,955 in after-tax cash inflow during 2014 (the $8,000 that didn't go to an RRSP less the $3,045 in additional taxes). So for five years, from 2014 until 2018, Pat has an extra $4,955 to work with.

Let's assume Pat invests that money in a TFSA that allows $5,500 a year. Because Pat has sworn off the stock market, the money is invested in 100% safe GICs returning 3% a year. The $4,955 a year growing at 3% a year for five years would build to a value of $26,575.

Pat and Jane will then be able to put $109,908 down on their home purchase in 2019 (the $83,333 they had from an inheritance, plus the $26,575 in the TFSA). Their mortgage would then be $223,425 (the purchase price of $333,333 less $109,908 down).

Their monthly mortgage payments over twenty-five years will be only $1,429.49 not $1,599.52. But just a minute, Pat and Jane want to eliminate their mortgage ASAP. They want to increase their mortgage payments to pay it down faster. So they leave the monthly payment amount at $1,599.52 and they add the $4,955 a year to the payments.

That is an additional $412.92 a month ($4,955/12 months). So instead of $1,599.52 they pay $2,012.44 a month ($1,599.52 plus $412.92), or $24,149.28 a year.

The mortgage would be paid off in thirteen years, not twenty-five. That would leave Pat mortgage-free in 2032 at age fifty-three. For the next twelve years, Pat makes RRSP contributions with the money that was going to the mortgage – $2,012.44 a month or $24,149.28 a year. Assuming Pat's marginal tax rate is still 38.1%, Pat will get a tax refund of $9,200.88 that first year that will also be contributed to his RRSP resulting in further tax refunds.

PAT'S TURBO-CHARGED RRSP

Let's look at Pat's turbo-charged RRSP assuming it grows at the same rate as the RRSP we have just looked at – average annual rate of return of 5%. Here's what that would build to for Pat in twelve years:

TABLE 8.7 The Tax Turbo-Charged RRSP

			The Tax Turbo-Charged RRSP				
Year	Pat's Age	RRSP Value 01-Jan	RRSP Cash Contri-bution	Tax Refund Prior Year Contribution	Total RRSP Contri-bution	Growth in RRSP (5% a yr)	RRSP Value 31-Dec
2032	53	$0	$24,149	$0	$24,149	$1,207	$25,356
2033	54	$25,356	$24,149	$9,201	$33,350	$2,935	$61,642
2034	55	$61,642	$24,149	$12,706	$36,855	$4,925	$103,422
2035	56	$103,422	$24,149	$14,042	$38,191	$7,081	$148,693
2036	57	$148,693	$24,149	$14,551	$38,700	$9,370	$196,762
2037	58	$196,762	$24,149	$14,745	$38,894	$11,783	$247,439
2038	59	$247,439	$24,149	$14,818	$38,967	$14,320	$300,727
2039	60	$300,727	$24,149	$14,847	$38,996	$16,986	$356,708
2040	61	$356,708	$24,149	$14,857	$39,006	$19,786	$415,500
2041	62	$415,500	$24,149	$14,861	$39,010	$22,726	$477,236
2042	63	$477,236	$24,149	$14,863	$39,012	$25,812	$542,061
2043	64	$542,061	$24,149	$14,864	$39,013	$29,054	$610,127
2044	65	$610,127	$24,149	$14,864	$39,013	$32,457	$681,597

In 2032 Pat contributes $24,149 (the amount that used to be going to the mortgage) and the next year receives a tax refund of 38.1% of that amount – $9,201. The next year, Pat puts in the regular $24,149 but also adds the tax refund from the prior year of $9,201 for a total contribution of $33,350. The opening RRSP value plus the total contribution for the year grows at the annual rate of 5%. This continues until he turns sixty-five.

As you can see, the "start late" strategy builds Pat's RRSP to $681,597. But to this we must add the original $55,000 Pat had in his RRSP in 2014. That amount, projected to 2044 at a 5% annual return, would build to $237,707. Pat's total RRSP will be worth $919,304, whereas the RRSP strategy from age thirty-five at 5% builds an RRSP of $769,218.

Pat would be further ahead by $150,086 with the Tax Turbo-Charged RRSP strategy.

CONCLUSION

Now it's your turn. Go to http://www.trahair.com, select "David's Books" on the left margin and click on the image of this book, and download the Money Maximizer for your own use. Then you can begin to make some real significant progress towards a worry-free retirement.

RETIRING WITHOUT THE STOCK MARKET

OK you're close to retirement, maybe in your late fifties or early sixties, and used to be pretty well set for your golden years. You worked your butt off and made RRSP contributions even during those years when doing so was very difficult.

You listened to the experts and trusted the stock market. You may have been talked into things like income trusts that you now know are usually high-risk equities.

Perhaps you even diversified geographically. Just like the experts recommended, you put money in the U.S. You put money in China. You also entered the emerging markets.

In a nutshell, you built a well-diversified portfolio of equities and fixed-income investments like government bonds.

And you still got clobbered.

Here's why. The following list from Bloomberg.com shows the returns of the major benchmark indexes for 2008, converted to Canadian dollars. Remember this is the return for the whole year, the return from the peak reached during June to the end of the year would be worse.

- S&P/TSX Composite Stock: −33.4%
- S&P 500 U.S. Stock: −22.61%

- NASDAQ U.S. Stock: −26.28%
- MSCI European and Asian Stock Market: −30.08%
- Emerging Countries Stock: −42.87%

You may even have been unfortunate enough to have had money in companies that went bankrupt. Or perhaps with an investment advisor that could not be trusted.

The sad truth is that your retirement nest egg has been severely damaged even five years after the crash.

Now what?

THE DEVASTATING EFFECT OF THE CRASH

Even most mutual fund salespeople agree that you should reduce your exposure to equities (the stock market) as you grow older. The reason is simple: if you don't you could get crunched financially.

Let's go back to the end of 2008. Say a seventy-year-old senior had 100% of his $200,000 portfolio invested in equity mutual funds that emulated the S&P/TSX Composite Index. As discussed earlier, during the period June of 2008 to March of 2009 the index lost almost 50% of its value. That means his $200,000 retirement nest egg got scalped by $100,000 − to only $100,000.

That's a tragedy. Now five years later he is still not even back to the $200,000 he had due to investment fees. What should he do now? Trust the stock market again? I don't think so.

WARNING: I have actually seen the following recommendation in print. I saw it in a book written by a well-know financial type, that you should take out a loan to invest in the stock market to make up for stock losses. Are you kidding me? You get decimated in the stock market, so you borrow money to try and make up for it? Give me a freakin' break.

ARE YOU GOING TO THROW GOOD MONEY AFTER BAD?

At this point you are probably still worried about your retirement plans.

Unfortunately, there is no magic solution to solve the problem. But surely you aren't going to trust the "system" to make up for what it has taken away are you?

If 2008 taught us anything, it was that people nearing retirement should have reduced their exposure to equities. Well, now is not the time to increase your exposure to them in the hopes of winning your money back. As far as I'm concerned, that's throwing good money after bad. It's gambling. It's risking personal financial disaster.

Here's my advice: get out of equities altogether if you can.

Given that we aren't going to trust the stock market to make up for what it took away, what is there that you can do to make your retirement a happy one?

Here are my thoughts.

YOU CAN STILL RETIRE WELL

You can't change the past and you can't control what the stock market does in the future. The key to retiring well is to forget about what you can't change or control and focus on what you can.

There are several vital factors that you still have control over, factors that with a little tweaking could add years to your retirement funding.

Let's bring back the Money Maximizer spreadsheet for Pat and Jane to see what the dollar value impact of each change is.

Throughout this chapter we'll use the basic situation described in the last chapter. Here's a summary of where we'll start:

- Pat is thirty-five and Jane is thirty in 2014.
- Pat has a job that paid $90,000 in salary in 2014 and that salary increases at 2% a year.
- Jane did not work and therefore made no payments into the CPP plan.
- Pat worked to age sixty-five in the year 2044.
- Pat's RRSP is worth $55,000 in 2014 and Pat makes RRSP contributions of $8,000 every year until retirement.
- Pat's RRSP grows at an average annual rate of return of 5% up to retirement and 4% thereafter.

- Inflation was assumed to be 2% per year.
- Pat and Jane were both eligible for the maximum OAS pension.
- Pat elects to start receiving the CPP pension at age sixty-five.
- Since Jane never works, she is not eligible for the CPP pension.
- Neither Pat nor Jane earn any other income after retirement (i.e., from self-employment or rental property, etc.).
- Pat and Jane estimate that they'll need 50% of Pat's pre-retirement income to maintain their standard of living after retirement.
- Pat and Jane live to age eighty-two.
- When Pat dies at age eighty-two in 2061, the balance in Pat's RRIF is transferred tax-free to Jane.
- Jane dies at age eighty-two in 2066.

The Money Maximizer shows that Pat and Jane's after-tax cash inflows will total $3,953,939 and that on a discounted basis the total is $1,449,155.

Those figures are from today – when Pat is only thirty-five.

We want to do some figuring for when Pat and Jane are close to retiring, so let's ignore the years from 2015 to 2039. Pat is now sixty and Jane is fifty-five. That's where we want to be – close to retirement. What happened in the past is water under the bridge.

Under the scenario just described for Pat and Jane, according to the Money Maximizer spreadsheet the total of their after-tax cash inflows from 2039 until they both cease to exist is $2,036,210. On a discounted basis the present value (in 2039 dollars) is $1,222,358. Keep these figures handy, as we'll be comparing them to the totals that different strategies result in. I'll call this the "base scenario."

Note that we'll build on the previous results. In other words, the most beneficial situation will be kept for the figures produced in the next section. For example, you'll see that CPP pension splitting makes sense in Pat and Jane's case. We'll assume they elect to split Pat's CPP pension income in making the next decision about whether to elect to receive the CPP early. Since you can use the Money Maximizer, you can decide to do it differently if you wish.

1. CPP Pension Splitting

As we have discussed, making sure you minimize your taxes through effective income splitting is paramount. This includes the CPP pension, RRIFs, annuitized RRSPs and any other pensions you may have.

Neither Pat or Jane has a company pension plan, but only Pat has paid into the CPP plan. What is the dollar impact of electing to split Pat's CPP pension income?

The total after-tax cash inflows increase to $2,088,844 and $1,248,198 on a discounted basis. That's an improvement of $52,634 and $25,840 respectively.

2. Electing CPP early

In this case, if Pat elects to start receiving CPP at age sixty and we input the early election penalty of 6.72% per year for 2014, total after-tax cash inflows are $2,030,618 and $1,259,655 on a discounted basis. Now that result is interesting. The total cash inflows are $58,226 lower than scenario 1, when Pat and Jane just split the CPP pension and waited until age sixty-five, but on a discounted basis, Pat and Jane are $11,457 further ahead.

That shows the unexpected results when you factor in taxes and the time value of money.

3. RRSP/RRIF Income Splitting

Pat has built up an RRSP – not a spousal RRSP – so all the RRSP and RRIF income that is received goes on Pat's income tax return. As we have seen, however, the pension income-splitting rules allow RRSP annuity income after age sixty-five and RRIF income to be split with a spouse or common-law partner.

Let's elect for Pat to split RRSP/RRIF income with Jane.

Pat and Jane's total after-tax cash inflows increase to $2,059,539 and $1,272,863 on a discounted basis. That's an improvement of $28,921 and $13,208 respectively, over scenario 2.

4. Extending Your Retirement Date

One of the best ways to set yourself up for a solid retirement is to delay your retirement date a little bit.

Even staying in the workforce for one extra year can have a huge impact on the number of years your retirement nest egg will last, because you are bringing in money instead of draining it, while your investments benefit from another year of growth.

What happens if Pat works just one additional year and instead of retiring at age sixty-five, makes it sixty-six?

Pat and Jane's total after-tax cash inflows increase to $2,216,462 and $1,349,619 on a discounted basis. That's an improvement of $156,923 and $76,756 respectively. As you can see this has the most significant impact of any of the other changes.

OTHER IDEAS

Spend less in retirement. In my experience, people tend to get more frugal as they age. This is a good thing for those who aren't naturally frugal, but the real penny pinchers are liable to hold back too much during retirement. What good is sacrificing your life to die with $1 million in the bank? On the other hand, there is real potential for the penny pinchers to teach the spenders how to get more for less when they are on a fixed income.

Make money in retirement. Even bringing in a few thousand dollars a year from a hobby or what you enjoy doing can bring a huge relief to the amount of money you'll need to stash away for retirement. Perhaps a rental property could provide a good cash flow. There are many creative ways to fund your retirement.

CONCLUSION

The investment peddlers used to tell us "just invest with me, and relax." Make a resolution not to believe them any longer. Don't throw any more good money after bad.

Retiring well is not going to be easy. But that's just the point – it never was.

YOU MAY NOT NEED AN RRSP

The simple truth about RRSPs is that for lower-income Canadians they don't make sense. First of all, they probably don't have any excess money after paying the bills to even make a contribution. Recommending that these people borrow to invest in an RRSP is simply irresponsible. Even if they have the money, the tax refund at a lower income bracket for many of these people will be pennies on the dollar. There are also other problems lurking like the clawback of government low-income subsidies because of RRSP investment values.

A COMMON MISCONCEPTION

Before we delve into the details, let me clear up one common misconception: RRSPs do not equal equities. RRSPs are registered plans that can hold many different things including equities (stocks or mutual funds that invest in stocks), bonds and GICs. An RRSP is therefore not "risky" by definition. It is if all you decide to put in it is equities, but not if you simply buy GICs in it. Don't confuse RRSPs with the actual investment instruments they may contain.

ALTERNATIVES TO RRSPs

Even if RRSPs make sense for a person, there are many alternatives: investing outside an RRSP, investing in real estate, investing in your own business, Tax-Free Savings Accounts (TFSAs), and possibly forming a corporation and leaving profits in at the low rate of tax and drawing dividends out after retirement.

But are any of these alternatives better than an RRSP?

INVESTING OUTSIDE VERSUS INSIDE AN RRSP

The debate over whether to invest inside or outside an RRSP has been going on for many years. If I sold investments for a living, I'd probably feed you a line we often hear: get the best of both worlds by maximizing your RRSP contribution *and* invest outside your RRSP!

Well, I don't sell investments. I know how tough it is to make even partial RRSP contributions after paying for the house, the kids, food and all the rest. I also know that if you can't maximize your RRSP contribution it's not the end of the world.

In fact, there are billions of dollars in unused RRSP contribution room – the amount that people could have contributed to their RRSP but didn't. You know what? Forget about it. It's not the major problem it's made out to be. For most people, maximizing their RRSP at all costs, even if they have to borrow, is the last thing they should do. It could lead to lots of debt and, as we saw in 2008, plummeting RRSP values. If that isn't a recipe for personal financial disaster I don't know what is.

OK enough said. But what do you do with the money you do have? To invest inside or outside an RRSP is the question. Here's my analysis of the issue.

We know that investing in RRSPs has two main benefits: the tax refund/deferral and the fact that the investments grow (hopefully!) on a tax-deferred basis. If all the stars align correctly, we will get a high tax break when we are working, our RRSP will grow and we will pay a lower rate of tax when we retire (since our income will be lower) and we will only have to pay it many years from now.

But there is one fly in the ointment. If we believe in the stock market and are using equities (stocks) in our RRSP, the capital gains when we sell the investments to take out retirement funds later are converted to income. In other words, in an RRSP you effectively pay tax on 100% of the gain between what you paid for the stock or mutual fund and what you sold it for.

This is not the case outside an RRSP, where you only pay tax on 50% of the capital gain (the 50% of the capital gain is called the "taxable capital gain").

Is the tax hit you take by holding equities in your RRSP enough to make investing outside an RRSP a better alternative?

Let's see. We'll use the following simple situation:

- original investment of $10,000 made January 1, 2014
- marginal tax rate of 46%
- annual growth rate of the investment is 6%
- investment growth compounds annually
- investment is cashed in after ten years, on December 31, 2023
- discount rate to factor in time value of money is 5%

We'll start with an RRSP and we'll assume the tax refund is received at the end of 2014, a year after the contribution was made.

It's vital that we factor in the value of the timing of the outflows and inflows. That shows the time value of money. Remember, $1 received today is worth more than $1 received a year from now.

Here are the results.

TABLE 10.1 Investing Inside an RRSP

RRSP	01- Jan 2014	31-Dec 2014	31-Dec 2023
Original investment (out) in	($10,000.00)		$17,908.48
Income tax refund (cost)		$4,600.00	($8,237.90)
Net after-tax (outflow) inflow	($10,000.00)	$4,600.00	$9,670.58
Present value at 5%			
Original investment	($10,000.00)		
Tax refund	$4,380.95		
Final after-tax amount	$5,936.90		
Total Net Present Value at 5%	$317.85		

At a 46% marginal tax bracket, a $10,000 RRSP contribution will yield a $4,600 tax refund.

The original $10,000 grows to $17,908.48 after ten years. That's an annual growth rate of 6% a year. (Take a calculator and punch in

10,000, then multiply by 1.06, get the result and keep doing that nine more times and you should get $17,908.48).

The tax on the withdrawal of $17,908.48 is 46% of the total (remember, there is no capital gains tax in an RRSP) and that's $8,237.90 of tax. The after-tax amount left is $9,670.58.

Here's the tricky part: we need to discount the $4,600 tax refund received a year from today and the $9,670.58 received ten years from now. Those present value figures are $4,380.95 and $5,936.90 respectively.

Add the outflows and inflows together and you'll find that the net present value of the outflows and inflows is $317.85 in today's dollars.

Now let's look at what would have happened if we invested the $10,000 in the same equities but outside an RRSP. Obviously there'd be no tax refund because there's no RRSP contribution, but how do the numbers shake out with the reduced tax on the capital gain? Here's that result.

TABLE 10.2   Investing Outside an RRSP

Invest Outside RRSP - Equities	01-Jan 2014	31-Dec 2023
Original investment (out) in	($10,000.00)	$17,908.48
Income tax cost		($1,818.95)
Net after-tax (outflow) inflow	($10,000.00)	$16,089.53
Present value at 5%		
Original investment	($10,000.00)	
Final after-tax amount	$9,877.57	
Total Net Present Value at 5%	($122.43)	

The income tax cost is calculated as follows: Proceeds of $17,908.48 less adjusted cost base (ACB) of $10,000 equals a capital gain of $7,908.48. The taxable capital gain is 50% of that or $3,954.24. Tax at 46% of $3,954.24 is $1,818.95.

That will leave cash in hand of $16,089.53. Discount that amount to today's dollars and you get $9,877.57.

Add the outflows and inflows together and the net present value of the outflows and inflows is ($122.43) – a negative figure – in today's dollars. That's $440.28 lower than the RRSP value of positive $317.85.

If I change the investment period to twenty years, the RRSP comes out ahead by $734.01. After thirty years, the RRSP comes out ahead by $792.28.

We obviously must be aware that each situation is different. There is also the issue around RRSPs having to convert into RRIFs that have minimum withdrawal requirements, whereas investments outside an RRSP can be cashed with little or no restrictions. Tax rates may also be higher or lower than this example.

But the key here is that we're comparing apples to apples. It is the same investment whether inside or outside an RRSP. We are also using the same discount rate in each case. Given that you should do your own specific calculations, it appears the math indicates a pretty consistent answer: investing in equities in an RRSP usually beats investing outside because of the huge benefit of an immediate tax refund.

The RRSP wins.

INVESTING IN REAL ESTATE

I was at the movies during the stock market crash and during the fifteen-minute sales pitch before the show there was an ad from a real estate company. It said in bold letters "The stock market has lost half its value. Invest in a sure thing: real estate."

Real estate is *not* a sure thing. The value of properties can, and often do, rise and fall just like the stock market.

You may be tempted to look at rental properties as a good investment. Rent it out and have the rental income cover the mortgage payments and operating costs, while the value of your investment increases. I have often thought that it may make sense for a real estate agent, who knows a particular area really well and could spot a bargain when it became available, to invest in a rental property rather than an RRSP.

It does make some logical sense. She would have an intimate knowledge of her investment and could keep an eye on it as she does her job.

But once again risk comes into play and in my opinion trumps the strategy. In this case, the real estate agent has the vast majority of her wealth in one thing: real estate. She has her home, her job and her rental property tied up in illiquid real estate investments. If the real estate market tanks, what happens? Possible job loss, maybe an inability to rent out the rental property, and the pressure of trying to keep up the mortgage payments on a principal residence and a rental property that may have both lost value.

Once again, seems too risky to me. The RRSP wins again.

INVESTING IN YOUR OWN BUSINESS

I have been self-employed for over twenty-five years. It's sometimes not easy, but I love it. I would not go back to a full-time job for double what I make now. There are many people that are in a similar position and they know what I know: it takes money to run a small business. What about investing in yourself, in your own business, instead of RRSPs?

Well, you'd run into the same problem as in the real estate idea – what if your business fails? You've lost everything by putting all your eggs in the one basket. Once again, diversifying your wealth by investing in an RRSP makes sense here, too.

Just before we leave this subject, however, I'd like to make another observation. I encourage you to try self-employment. There is no such thing as a job-for-life anymore. Even pension plans can go bankrupt. Unfortunately you could get the axe any day.

Protect yourself. At least try self-employment on a part-time basis to see how it fits. You may need to find work at a later time to help pay the bills.

Your only protection is to educate yourself. Make yourself marketable by learning how to do what you love and make money doing it.

INVEST IN A TAX-FREE SAVINGS ACCOUNT

Is a Tax-Free Savings Account (TFSA) a good alternative to an RRSP? Let's find out.

Beginning in January 2009 you could contribute $5,000 per year. Since January 2013 you can put up to $5,500 per year into this type of plan and the income (interest, dividends, capital gains, etc.) that is earned on the contributions is never taxed. The TFSA is available to any Canadian resident individual (other than trusts) eighteen years of age and older.

Main Features of the TFSA:

- Generally you are allowed to invest in the same products that qualify for investments in your RRSP.
- Unused contribution room will be carried forward indefinitely.
- The CRA states that it will determine the contribution room for each individual who files a personal income tax return.
- Any withdrawals will be added to the contribution room for the following year.
- The contribution room is indexed to inflation, rounded to the nearest $500.
- Interest on money borrowed to make a contribution is not deductible for tax purposes.
- Losses in a TFSA cannot be used to offset gains or income earned outside a TFSA.
- Upon death, there is a deemed disposition (it's treated like you cashed it in) just prior to the death, so accumulated income and capital gains that were earned up to the date of death are tax-exempt.
- The plan can be left to a surviving spouse and maintain its tax-exempt status, or can be transferred to the surviving spouse's plan without affecting the spouse's contribution room.
- Upon a marriage breakdown, transfers are allowed to the former spouse's plan and this will not increase the amount of contribution room of the transferor or reduce the contribution room of the transferee.
- For non-residents, existing plans will continue to be tax-exempt, no contributions will be allowed while non-resident and no contribution room will accrue while non-resident.
- The TFSA can be used as collateral for a loan.
- There will be a 1% tax on excess contributions, similar to other registered plans.

This plan is especially important if you are conservative like me. In fact, in my opinion, as I have said many times before, when it comes to personal finances you should not risk the farm. That means staying out of the stock market.

We've already discussed how anyone who trusted the TSX with their house deposit money may have seen it drop by 50% in 2008/2009. That's why it makes more sense to stick to the strategy – invest only in no-risk, no-fee, government-guaranteed investments like GICs, term deposits and high-income savings accounts.

When held in regular (non-RRSP, non-TFSA) investment accounts, however, the interest on our no-risk products are taxed each and every year at our marginal tax rate (the rate at which each additional dollar is taxed, given all your other income and deductions). That's one of the main benefits of the TFSA – no income tax on the earnings.

The other tax advantage is that the withdrawals from the TFSA are not included in income or used for federal income-tested benefits like the Canada Child Tax Benefit (CCTB), Employment Insurance (EI), the Goods and Services Tax Credit (GSTC), the Guaranteed Income Supplement (GIS), the Working Income Tax Benefit (WITB) or the clawback of Old Age Security (OAS).

THE TFSA AS AN INCOME SPLITTER

Remember our friend income splitting to reduce our family tax bill? Well, the TFSA is ideal for anyone with kids eighteen years of age or older or a non-working spouse. That's because there is no "attribution" of income to you when you give funds to your family members to contribute to their TFSA.

In other words, if you give $5,500 to your spouse and he or she invests in a GIC or other investment outside a TFSA, the income (and any dividends) earned on that $5,500 must be reported on your, not his or her, income tax return. The income "attributes" back to you because it was your $5,500 to begin with. That's not the case with the TFSA. With a TFSA the interest earned would not be reported, period.

OPPORTUNITY FOR RETIREES

Since there is no upper age limit for contributors, there is an opportunity for retired people that are no longer able to make RRSP contributions to reduce their taxes. For example, if you are over seventy-one and already drawing from your RRIF account, you could invest $5,500 per year in a TFSA to stop the taxation of the income on it.

DOES ANYONE HAVE $5,500 OUTSIDE A REGISTERED ACCOUNT?

In fact, anyone who already has $5,500 invested outside a registered account like an RRSP can transfer the investment to a TFSA and immediately stop the taxation of the income on the account. This is called a "transfer-in-kind."

This is ideal for fixed-income products like GICs, but you'll need to be careful with other investments like stocks and mutual funds. That's because you'll be deemed to have disposed of the investment at its Fair Market Value (FMV) at the time of the transfer. Any inherent gains to that point will have to be reported on your tax return.

Here's the catch: any capital losses will be deemed to be nil on a transfer of a losing stock or mutual fund to a TFSA. The solution to this is to sell the loser before the transfer and then put the $5,500 into the TFSA through a separate transaction.

WHY THE TFSA IS BETTER THAN AN RRSP FOR HOME BUYERS

The TFSA is a registered plan like an RRSP but is very different than an RRSP in that contributions to the TFSA are not tax deductible. The flip side of this is that withdrawals from the TFSA are not taxable, and that includes any income earned in the plan.

This plan is ideal for saving for a house deposit, even better than an RRSP Home Buyers' Plan, for several reasons.

First of all, unlike an RRSP, you don't have to have "earned income" to create room for the contribution – everyone gets $5,500 per year starting at age eighteen. With an RRSP you need earned income (basically a salary or self-employment earnings) to create RRSP room. For example, say you are twenty-one and have just graduated from University in 2014. You make $20,000 during the rest of your graduating year. Your RRSP contribution room for the next year (2015) is $3,600 (18% of your prior year's earned income of $20,000).

With the TFSA, your limit would be $26,500 by 2015 since you turned eighteen in 2011. Let's say you have your eye on a home that will cost $130,000 and that you'd like to put down a minimum deposit of 15% ($19,500). With the TFSA, you would be able to do that by 2015. With an RRSP you'd have to wait until your earned income had totaled $108,333 to create $19,500 of RRSP room, since 18% of $108,333 is $19,500.

But there are more problems with an RRSP. First of all, when you are just starting out in the job market, your income is likely to be low. You are therefore in a low tax bracket and your RRSP contributions result in a low refund. For example, if your salary is between $18,503 and $40,120 in Ontario in 2014 your tax bracket was only 20.05%. In other words, a $10,000 RRSP contribution would result in a $2,005 refund. Good but not great.

THE RRSP HOME BUYERS' PLAN

The RRSP Home Buyers' Plan (HBP) allows first-time home buyers to withdraw up to $25,000 from their RRSP to purchase or build a qualifying home. This withdrawal is not taxed immediately and your RRSP issuer will not withhold tax on the amount, but there is a catch: the full amount must be repaid to your RRSP within fifteen years.

In other words, if you withdrew $25,000, $1,667 must be repaid to your RRSP each year for fifteen years or the required repayment amount ($1,667) is added to your taxable income so you'll have to pay income tax on it. This is the difficulty with the HBP. Once you have assumed responsibility for carrying a mortgage, you'll feel the pressure of making those mortgage payments and paying property taxes, repairs and maintenance, etc., on your home. You may find that coming up with $1,667 to replenish your RRSP each and every year may be difficult.

It would seem to me that you would be better off using a TFSA from the beginning to save for your home deposit.

If you are past this stage and have already invested in RRSPs and do not have savings outside your RRSP, using the HBP to invest in a home at the right time makes sense, since it's the only way you'll get that deposit and consequently your home.

KEEPING PROFITS IN A CORPORATION

If you have your own business that is incorporated, you may wish to consider using it as a tax deferral mechanism. Basically, the profits of an active business corporation are taxed in the company at a low rate of tax – approximately 15%, in most cases. The low rate is meant to benefit small business owners by leaving more after-tax money in the corporation, enabling it to grow by investing in new equipment or hiring new people for example.

You as the owner/shareholder are not taxed personally on corporate profits until you take the money out. If you take out all the profits as salary, you pay tax as a normal employee would, at whatever marginal tax rate you fall into. The salary expense to the corporation would then leave it with no profit to tax at the low rate. This effectively eliminates the advantage of the low corporate rate of income tax.

If, however, you don't need to take all the profits out, you can leave them in the corporation and pay tax at the low rate. Then, years later when you retire, you can then withdraw the profits as dividends at a reduced personal tax rate. This is similar to what an RRSP does.

Once again this strategy runs the risk of putting all your eggs in one basket. The business could suffer some lean years or even go under. There are also issues related to the taxation of the investment income in the corporation not being active income subject to the low rate of tax. But if structured correctly it may be something worth considering.

CONCLUSION

The alternatives to a simple RRSP have one major problem: it's hard to beat the tax deferral that an RRSP provides, especially for higher income people.

And there are other problems with ignoring RRSPs. With alternative strategies like putting all your money in real estate, there is the problem of a lack of diversification. A downturn in the housing market when your home and your job, as well as your rental property, all depend on the housing market remaining solid is simply too risky.

The same can be said for investing in your own business.

Remember point number one of the Antidote: avoid personal financial disasters. Putting all your eggs in one basket like real estate or self-employment puts you in a situation with the potential for personal financial disaster. Don't do it.

In fact, why even consider alternatives to an RRSP when you can use one to diversify your wealth, and it allows you to invest in 100% safe GICs that will never decline and are guaranteed by the federal government (through CDIC) even if the financial institution that issues them goes under?

Combine those benefits with the Tax Turbo-Charged RRSP strategy that allows you to start late and use the significant tax benefit of making RRSP contributions during your peak earnings years, and you've got a winning strategy.

11

THE ANTIDOTE SUMMARY

OK, you've hung in there for the whole book. Here's a summary of The Antidote. Follow it and you can rest easy, knowing that your retirement nest egg will never decline even if your bank goes under.

1. AVOID PERSONAL FINANCIAL DISASTERS

- Never touch anything that cannot be simply explained to you in plain English.
- Don't invest in anything that is not guaranteed by the government.
- Never borrow to invest.
- Avoid complicated investment schemes. If it sounds too good to be true, it is.

2. YOU DON'T NEED THE STOCK MARKET OR MUTUAL FUNDS

- The truth is that you don't need to risk your hard-earned money in the stock market and you don't need mutual funds.
- You can use 100% government-guaranteed investment certificates to achieve your goals without the risk of losing your shirt.
- If you want to take a chance, buy a lottery ticket.

3. BUY A HOME AND PAY OFF THE MORTGAGE

- Decide if you can afford a house and, if you can, buy one.
- Do the calculation of how many years it will take to pay off the mortgage and do it before you retire.
- Never risk your home for any kind of investment idea, no matter what.

4. REDUCING EXPENSES DOESN'T HAVE TO BE PAINFUL

- Focus on two of your biggest expenses – income taxes and interest on your debt.
- Pay to have your family's personal income tax returns prepared by a qualified expert.
- Pay extra to have that expert analyze your family situation to minimize your tax bill by income splitting, etc.
- Find out what your credit rating is and improve it.
- Get at least three quotes on any debt that you get into.

5. FORGET RRSPs UNTIL YOUR DEBT IS PAID OFF (THE OPPORTUNITY ZONE)

- Do not even think about saving for retirement until you have paid off student loans and bought a home.
- Pay off the mortgage before investing another dime in an RRSP.
- Never borrow to invest in an RRSP.

6. ASK YOURSELF IF YOU REALLY NEED AN INVESTMENT ADVISOR

- If you've got a bad one, find a good one.
- If you can't find a good one, simplify your finances so you don't need one at all.

INDEX

INDEX